Because He Could

The Story Behind Youth Formula

Marlies White

Published by Somalife, January 2021
ISBN: 9781777517809

Editor: Danielle Anderson
Typeset: Greg Salisbury
Book Cover Design: Tara Eymundson
Portrait Photographer: Marianne Hardy

DISCLAIMER: This book is a memoir. It reflects the author's present recollections of experiences over time. Several names have been changed to protect the guilty.

Contents

This book is dedicated to my stalwart friend, Emilienne Hardy, who I have been privileged to know for the past two decades. Since the early 2000's, our dragon boating days, Emily has always been there for me when I needed a listening ear. With her wealth of wisdom, she gave me much support and good counsel, when I was going through dark times. I will be forever grateful to Emily, as I knew I was never alone while I had her in my life.

Baby Cakes…this book is dedicated to you,
with much love… Marlies

Introduction

"Those who overcome great challenges will be changed, and often in unexpected ways. For our struggles enter our lives as unwelcome guests, but they bring valuable gifts. And once the pain subsides, the gifts remain. These gifts are life's true treasures, bought at great price, but cannot be acquired in any other way."
—**Steve Goodier**

The world is an ever-changing place—a statement that is truer now than ever before. Progress is marching forward at an accelerating pace, and volumes upon volumes have been filled with the marvels of modern technology. Mankind continuously searches for and creates ways to live longer, healthier, happier lives, and part of this has been the never-ending search for the fountain of youth. Since the beginning of time, this elusive target has evaded capture by even the most brilliant of men—that is, until now.

One of the crowning achievements of my life has been my involvement in the creation of SomaLife's Youth Formula, developed by my late husband Dr. Philip White. This product has changed the lives of so many people, myself included, and I am honoured to be involved in bringing it into the world. However, the man who created it, while brilliant, was also incredibly flawed. There were decisions he made that brought a lot of turmoil into our lives, and I had to overcome many obstacles and make some very challenging decisions about how to move forward. Writing this book has forced me to be introspective, and I can now see why some things happened the way that they did. I can also see how I could have done things differently, but at the moment I'm not sure that I would change anything even if I could. While there was a lot of pain and frustration, every step I took brought me to where I am today. I feel such a great appreciation and gratitude for life in general and particularly for having been given the tools to make a difference in the lives of others.

Looking back now, I can finally come to grips with how my life unfolded. While there was a lot of drama and heartbreak along the way, it brought me to the new and wonderfully happy state I find myself in today. By telling my story, I hope to share the message that you are the only one

in control of your life, and that it is your choices that determine how you move forward and what the consequences will be. I also want to show you that staying focused on a passion can get you through the dark times and bring you to a place where the sun may shine for you again.

"Some of the most beautiful things worth having in your life come wrapped in a crown of thorns."
-**Shannon L. Alder**

ONE

The Beginning

My story started in Lübeck, Germany. It is a city of beauty and intellect associated with three Nobel laureates: Günter Grass, Thomas Mann, and Willy Brandt. Surrounded by water, the old town brings to life one thousand years of history with its seven towers and five principal churches. But when you are visiting, what's really important is that you taste and pay homage to the city's speciality: Lübeck's famous marzipan, which has been the sweetest temptation for as long as there have been almonds.

I was born to Emma and Albert Hennings in 1948, not long after WWII had ended. Times were still hard in Germany; food was rationed, with butter and sugar being in particularly limited supply. My mom has told me that in those early years of my life, they sometimes made soup out of pared potato peelings so as to stretch their food a little further. However, I was too young to remember much of that.

In 1954, just as I was reaching my sixth birthday, my parents made the courageous decision to emigrate to Canada with me and my brother, who was five years older. Germany was still rebuilding after the many bombings and the future looked bleak, so Canada became our hope of a better life. Funds for a move like this were not readily available to my parents in the way of savings, so our church in Germany loaned us the money we needed to move to a German community in Alberta.

I still remember the boat trip from Germany to Canada on the Arosa Star. My brother and mom were deathly ill, being severely seasick, so my dad and I stayed outdoors on deck. I recall eating bananas to stave off becoming ill myself as they helped keep my stomach settled. Other than that, the voyage was uneventful. After we arrived at port, we took a long train trip through the beautiful countryside to settle in Camrose, Alberta, where we all began to slowly integrate into this country we would now call home.

I started Grade One without knowing a word of English. Thankfully, my first-ever teacher, Mrs. Hammer, was very kind—I remember her fondly to this day. I recall being asked to write my name on the blackboard, I suppose to introduce myself to the rest of the class, but I didn't understand what was being asked of me. Eventually I figured it out, and I proceeded to spell my name in all capital letters—as kids do when they are first learning to print. Mrs. Hammer rewrote it on the board as "Marlies," with lower-case letters, and I remember telling her that wasn't the right way to spell it; in my mind my name should have been all in capitals. That is what I had been taught. I was a rebel for the first time—and here I have to smile, because I have never been a rebel. Youngsters learn quickly, though, and I was soon accepted by my peers.

There was not a social assistance net for immigrants back then as there is now, so for my parents it was sink or swim. Jobs in Camrose were scarce, and although my mother found work as a cleaning lady with a lovely family who treated her well, it wasn't enough income to maintain a basic quality of life for us. So, my father left Camrose with a friend who had an old truck in order to look for work. They headed for Victoria, BC, but their truck broke down as they were nearing Kelowna. Fortunately, we had some distant relatives there who took my father in.

In 1954, Kelowna—which is situated midway on a ninety-mile-long lake—only had a population of about twenty thousand people. It was a little jewel in the Okanagan Valley, and I think Dad fell in love with it immediately.

Although he had been a leather master in Germany, Dad was prepared to take any job available. He quickly found work as a farm labourer with the Buckland family in Rutland, a nearby town which has now become part of Kelowna. Rutland turned out to be a great place for my family to settle—we had relatives close by, there was a German Grace Baptist Church we could attend, and we were given a small apartment over the garage at the Buckland Orchards Farm to live in. Soon my dad was able to send for us, and before the next school year my mom, my brother, and I arrived by train.

While we were a little better established in Rutland and had a roof over our heads, our furnishings were still very sparse. I recall Mom using small apple boxes as dish cabinets with tea towels over the openings to hide the contents. We didn't have much, but my parents always made the best of what we had.

Our new home was just under three miles from Rutland Elementary, and you had to live at least three miles from the school to be picked up by the bus. So, on the first day of classes my mom walked me to school to teach me how to get there. There were two ways you could go: one offered a moderate incline but was long and winding, the other a shorter route that in places seemed to be on a ninety degree angle. In the end, I ended up going whichever way the other kids who lived nearby would go.

I had finished Grade One without incident, but Grade Two brought with it some of the first instances of bullying—an introduction to the types of kids I would encounter throughout the rest of my time in school. Some of my classmates took advantage of my lack of knowledge around some of the local customs to convince me to do things I wasn't aware I shouldn't. Even at age six, kids can be unkind at the very least, and unfortunately my experiences with bullying only got worse as I got older. There is no excuse for this type of behaviour, ever! However, the upside of these experiences is that they have allowed me to relate to other people going through the same thing.

Thankfully, life at home was a little better—we seemed to have angels looking after the big things in our lives. The family my mom had been cleaning house for in Alberta referred her to a relative of theirs in Kelowna, and once again she found a really nice family to work for, the Bennetts, who owned Palace Meat Market on the main street in town. This couple then introduced Mom to Jack Krimmer, and then she had two houses to clean. After Mom had been working for Mr. Krimmer for several years, he offered to sell us a three-acre parcel of land with some old empty buildings on it for nine hundred dollars and allowed them to make payments on it instead of having to buy it outright—something that is unheard of today.

Next came many days and evenings when my dad—with the help of my mom and brother—worked on turning one of the buildings into our first home. The dwelling was very primitive, without even an inside bathroom. Televisions were not very common yet, and even if they had been, we had no electricity. Instead, we would stay up as late as we could by lighting a kerosene lamp and listening to stories on the battery powered radio. We had a hand pump in the kitchen that brought up water from a well my father had dug on the property. The stove was one that burned sawdust, dispensed from a hopper on the side of the stove, and we kept it running most of the time. When temperatures dropped in the winter and snow lay on the ground, Mom would open the oven door in the morning to warm our clothes, hung over a chair, before we had to go to school. Kids these days would have no idea how to survive without all the niceties they have now, but all the hardships we faced back then strengthened our character, and we were still able to build a life.

Our new property was about five or six miles away from the Buckland farm, which meant Dad now needed to drive to work. So, in the midfifties we got our first car which gave our family more flexibility. My dad drove to his job, and my mother would either take the bus to her cleaning jobs or ride a bicycle seven or so miles—she had never learned to drive a car and did not get her license until she was in her fifties. If I wasn't in school I would ride my bike to her jobs with her, and it was on one of these rides, when I was almost ten, that she told me I was going to have a brother or sister. I don't recall being impressed or excited either way; I had always been happy with just having an older brother and a father who adored me.

My sister arrived in 1958 and she was a cute little kid, but with such a large age gap between us we never developed a close relationship. I remember that when she was around three or four, she wouldn't go to bed unless I went as well, and as a teenager at the time I resented her for that. Now that we are both adults, we have a great time when we are together, but unfortunately that doesn't happen very often. Distance still stops us from creating that close sisterly bond.

My parents now had an extra mouth to feed, and money was often tight. My dad was making just seventy-five cents an hour, and even with Mom working, sometimes buying enough groceries to put food on the table was a real challenge. My mom had to be creative about finding ways to make meals with very little—the saying "making a silk purse out of a sow's ear" often comes to mind. I'm sure she was grateful that the Schmidts, who attended our church and owned Top Hat Grocery, allowed her to carry a small account with them as there were no food banks available. It was during this time of my life that I began to understand that you don't spend what you don't have, and that debt must always be taken care of before you spend on anything else. My parents never bought anything—other than necessities such as food and the land to build a home—unless they could pay for it in cash. To their dying day, they never once used a credit card.

My school experience was pretty average for the most part, and I kept busy by joining many activities such as sports, drama, photography, and the student council. I had above average grades in most subjects, but in Grade Eleven the wheels fell off the wagon. That year I had a social studies class where I found the teacher so boring that I just couldn't get interested in the material. So, I didn't study. As the year went on, I became fairly certain that I would fail the last exam and thus fail Grade Eleven and be left behind. At the age of almost seventeen—just a month and a half before the end of the school year—I made the decision to quit. I don't know whether I would have passed or failed school if I had stuck it out, but I'm not sure it mattered either way, as my parents couldn't afford to send me to university.

Thankfully, my math teacher, Mr. Drinkwater, would not let me just walk out of school without a plan. He called the hairdressing school in Vernon, BC, and set up an appointment for me to be interviewed to get into the next training class. I was offered a spot, but the school was thirty miles away from home which meant that I couldn't commute each day. Luckily my parents had church friends in the area who had a daughter my age, and they were willing to let me to live with them for six months to take this course. So, off I went. I am sure that sending me to hairdressing school and having to pay my room and board put a financial burden on my parents, so I would give mom her perms and cut my dad's hair on a regular basis to pay them back in this small way.

Once I finished the training in 1965, I went off to find work as an apprentice until I turned eighteen and could write the exam to become a full-fledged hairdresser. My first job paid me seventeen dollars a week for sweeping up hair and other cleaning duties, but I was anxious to get into creating hairstyles and cutting hair—something I turned out to be really good at. I wanted to be able to get to work without depending on friends or a bus, so I bought my first car: a 1949 Vanguard. It had a broken starter motor, but the car was only twenty-five dollars and the body was good. My dad told me I was crazy to buy this car and that I would break my arm trying to start it, but he still showed me how to crank it properly. I never did break an arm, although I was embarrassed enough to park somewhere out of the way so that no one could see me start it.

Once I turned eighteen and passed my hairdresser exam, I moved to a nicer salon and finally started building a clientele of my own. Now I was making fifty dollars a week AND commissions. I left home and moved into a room in a house just around the corner from my work.

One day, my boss came to me and offered me an interesting opportunity. One of the local funeral homes had asked him to come do hairdos for women who were to have an open casket viewing at their funeral, and as he was really nervous about doing this, he asked if I would take this on. It paid seven dollars per hairdo—at that time, a haircut was only $1.50, and a full perm and style cost $10—so I agreed as it would make a real difference in my budgeting. I generally didn't mind doing this work, although it could be disturbing when I saw people I knew. I saw one of my classmates who had been in a rollover in his VW—seatbelts had not come out yet, so the only marks on him were the imprint of the steering wheel on his chest and a scratch across his nose. Another one was a girl I had been on a double date with. She was a barrel racer, and when her horse fell, he had stepped on the side of her face getting up. I had to do her hair as best I could to hide those marks. The most tragic one was a seven-year-old who had drowned—he looked peacefully asleep, but I knew he wasn't ever going to wake up. It was a sad job, but I felt I was doing a good service by making these people look their best for their final journey.

Back at the salon, I was having a great time and built a good clientele. However, when I was nineteen years old I got wanderlust and wanted to be somewhere else. I found a job as a hairdresser in Prince Rupert, about a two-day drive northwest of Kelowna, and set off on my own... sort of. I had found a room to rent with a nice older couple, and one night they invited me to a church dinner. It was there I met David, who had just arrived from England to teach in a local high school. He was absolutely gorgeous and had a beautiful accent, and we soon began to date.

Within a year of arriving in Prince Rupert, my career as a hairdresser came to an abrupt end. While doing hair for a wedding party, we discovered that every single one of these women had lice. Unfortunately for them, we had to stop what we were doing, contact a health inspector, and then carefully disinfect the whole salon. At that point I quit hairdressing as I wasn't getting paid enough to have to deal with lice, and this whole event had a huge gross-out factor. I then had a brief and unsuccessful stint as a telephone operator—this was back when you sat in front of a huge board and plugged wires in to make a connection—before moving on to become a bank teller. After three career moves in such a short space of time, I felt I had finally found my niche. I wasn't a math genius, but I enjoyed the numbers and liked meeting new people every day.

Throughout all these career changes my relationship with David deepened, and after some months he asked me to marry him. I loved him, a lot, and at almost twenty I thought it was time—in those days you married young. So, I said yes. I went back to live with my parents to prepare for the wedding, and we got married on July 13, 1968. We went on a honeymoon to a quaint little resort in the Gulf Islands before making our way back to Prince Rupert.

As a high school dropout, I thought I was so lucky to have married such an educated man; little did I know the troubles that were to come.

TWO

Marriage Number One

When we arrived in Prince Rupert, we had to find a place to rent but were short on money after the wedding and the travel. David went to the bank to borrow twenty-five dollars to get us through to his first paycheck—the equivalent of about two hundred dollars today—and the bank gave him an unsecured loan for that amount. Oh, how times have changed!

We rented a basement suite, and I started to learn how to cook. I had not enjoyed home economics class in school at all, once again due to the teacher—I know now that it is the quality of the teacher and how they teach that determines their students' success—so I had a lot to learn and made many mistakes along the way. One Sunday I proudly whipped up a batch of pancakes and inadvertently made enough to feed a small army, so we asked all the other tenants in the house to join us for breakfast. My cooking skills have great improved since then, although I still just make comfortable, home-style cooking.

During those early days, David and I had many wonderful times together. We would go skiing with friends at a hill down the road, and many evenings were spent playing cards with other teachers. Life in the north was pretty good, but it wasn't long before the cracks in our marriage began to show.

Because David was such an attractive man, I always felt

other women showed too much interest in him. When I would bring up how uncomfortable this made me, he would quickly become angry. One day, we got into an argument about how his female coworkers saw him and their overt advances. I accused him of not being clear with them about being married, and he took umbrage to that. The argument escalated until David drove his fist through the hall door. This was my first taste of his lack of impulse control.

This pattern continued throughout our first year of marriage. Most of the time he was loving and fun to be with, but when he got angry, he at times became physical. He once even punched me in the face, sending me to the hospital with what I thought might be a broken jaw. I had never seen my father raise his hand to my mother, so this was something new to me. I ended up blaming myself to some extent; I thought that if I wasn't so outspoken, I could keep the boat from rocking.

The only friends we had were David's colleagues from school, so I decided to join the Little Theatre group to make my own friends. The best time in all of this was getting to play the part of Marilyn Monroe in *The Seven Year Itch*. I loved being part of the theatre; I could be beautiful in a make-believe world.

At the end of the school year, David wanted to move back to England for a year so that I could meet his family. So, in the summer of 1969 we packed up and flew over to start a new chapter of our lives. He began teaching at a school in his hometown while I signed up with a temp agency and got hired as an office worker in a metal manufacturing plant. Although my time there was meant to be temporary, they offered me a full-time position—I suppose I had proven my worth. My greatest achievement there was when the paymaster went on a two-week vacation and the company asked me, a newcomer, to step in and do the payroll for about fifty warehouse workers and ten office staff. I don't know why they didn't choose one of the existing employees as I was still learning the monetary system—there were pounds, shillings, and pence, as well as a guinea which was equal to one pound and one pence. It was all so confusing. But I took this onerous task on, and I managed to do it without a single mistake.

While I enjoyed my work, I was eager to return to Canada—I couldn't imagine living in the UK for any length of time, particularly with the lack of central heating. During the cold, damp winter, we would sit in our tiny living room in front of a little fire, which was fed by coal that had to be shovelled and then brought into the house. The fire would keep the front of me warm, but my back would be freezing.

Having a bath was also an adventure. We had to put shillings into an electric meter to get hot water from an Ascot heater hanging up on the wall above the tub. The only good thing about feeding shillings into this heater was when the meter reader would come and give back some of the shillings for overpayment. Of course, sometimes the shillings would run out and the lights would go off. Then one of us would have to trek to the pub around the corner and ask them to trade us some shillings for a pound note so that we could get things going again.

As the end of the year approached, David hadn't received any confirmation that he had a teaching job to come back to in Canada. In order to resolve this dilemma, he started an affair with a married coworker. I believe he wanted someone to hang on to if moving back to Canada didn't pan out, so by having an affair, all was well in his world—key word HIS.

David told me about the tryst shortly after it happened— I'm not even sure why, as I had no way of knowing about his infidelity. After he confessed, I went into the bathroom and cried my eyes out. I was heartbroken. This was all too much for me. I was only twenty-two years old, far from home, vulnerable, and afraid for the future. I wanted to die. I was in the bathroom for hours, contemplating the changed state of my world and his betrayal, and David didn't even bother to check on me to ask if I was okay. That should have been a wake-up call.

I told him to end the affair, and he agreed. But when I drove to the school to pick David up the following day, I arrived to find them both standing by her car and talking. Who knows, maybe he was saying goodbye. As I drove into the schoolyard, I wanted nothing more than to T-bone her car—I was that angry!

Later that night, I called my mom long distance and asked if I could stay with her and Dad if I came back to Canada without David. Without me having to go into any detail, she said, "Of course." Just knowing that no questions would be asked gave me a great sense of relief, and at that point I knew I would find a way to get back home.

The next few months were messy, especially as I felt I had no one I could go to for emotional support. David's parents were made aware of what had transpired, and their solution was to essentially tell me that what he had done wasn't a big deal and to get over it. Finally a job offer came through, and David and I returned to Canada together to settle once again in Kelowna. However, I knew that things would never be the same between us. My life and feelings for him had changed; you can forgive, but it is hard to forget.

As the years went by, there were good times and bad times. David's impulse-control issues continued to manifest with him becoming physical, throwing things at me, or punching me, yet I still stuck by him. We thought of starting a family at one point, but I had been suffering from endometriosis throughout our marriage and it became so painful that my doctor recommended surgery to alleviate this problem. After I woke from the surgery, I was told that I had so many fibroids and it was such a mess inside that they did an oophorectomy, which meant that both my ovaries were removed as well as my uterus. I could now never have children on my own or even by way of a surrogate mother. I felt a great sadness for this loss. I also felt that I would now be less of a woman in my husband's eyes—that he would no longer feel an attraction for me—and there were times when I thought I could see this in his eyes. Despite all of this, choosing to leave felt like I would be failing myself, our marriage, and my own family, and so I hung in there.

Strangely enough, the final straw came when David did not come home to celebrate our fifteenth wedding anniversary. He was taking some university courses out on the coast to get his master's degree in education and had been gone for the better part of a month. Our anniversary fell on a weekend that year, and he was just a four-hour drive from home. Maybe it was unreasonable on my part, but the fact that he wouldn't make the effort to come home made me feel completely unimportant to him.

After fifteen years of living on this roller coaster, I finally got the courage to leave and start a new chapter in my life. I didn't know what lay ahead of me, but I hoped it would be better than what I was leaving behind.

THREE

Single Life

In 1983, I found myself settling into life as a single woman. After I "ran away from home," I initially stayed with my brother and his family for three nights before finding a basement suite where I lived for about six months. However, David kept tabs on me—he was unhappy that I had left—and I didn't feel comfortable being that easily accessible, so I moved into an apartment building with a secure front door and lobby. Even that did not deter him, and at one point I had to call the police and ask them to remove him from the front of the building as he was causing a disturbance. He was finally starting to get the picture that I would not be coming home. I then made the decision to buy a mobile home in a park that had an age restriction of having to be at least forty-five years old. I was only thirty-five at the time, but I asked them to make an exception and they did. After a couple of years in the mobile home, I moved into a cute little house that had been renovated by an artist and his mother, and I was happy living there in my own space. Every move I made brought me closer to what I had lost in a material sense since leaving David.

I was now in the final throes of my divorce, and I was almost free. Being single again was a lot of fun at times, yet I still wondered what would come next.

And then, I met Philip White.

Philip was a family doctor with a passion for research. He had been referred to me by a mutual acquaintance to acquire a small loan—I had continued to work in the bank throughout my marriage and had worked my way up to become an account manager for loans, mortgages, and investments—and we instantly hit it off. He was "sort of" separated but still married to his wife of fifteen years, with two pre-teen sons still living at home. He was dashing, exciting, and made me feel like I was on top of the world—sometimes literally. He was a pilot as well as a doctor, and we often took to the skies on the weekends.

At first, I thought that this would be a harmless friendship. I was just his banker, and he was just allowing me to share his passion of flying. Soon, though, I fell in love with him. He seemed to be so different from David—so happy and loving. Every time he visited me, he always said how good it was to see me with a huge grin on his face, and I felt he really meant it. Looking back now, though, I can see that I was wrong to get involved with him while he was still technically a married man. As the saying goes, hindsight is 20/20!

Although Philip stated his marriage was over, he was reluctant to leave his wife as he still had two sons at home—he wanted to wait until they were a little older before he officially severed ties with their mother. He moved in and out of his home for two or three years before he finally moved in with me. All in all, it took him six years after I met him to apply for his divorce. Although I hated living in this limbo, I had to give him credit for thinking about his sons and the impact a divorce would have had on them—but in the end, it had the same impact anyway. His sons were not happy with the divorce, and I could tell they blamed me. Eventually they came around, though, and today we enjoy a good relationship.

Despite these frustrations, life with Philip could be quite

exciting, and as our relationship developed, I became more and more interested in being a part of his passion for flying. So, I put my fear of flying aside and managed to get my pilot's license. I vividly remember my initial training flight with my instructor. The plane vibrated as we raced down the runway, getting ready to lift off. It felt like the bottom would drop out at any minute. I was scared, but I did my best to calm myself down and push through.

While I was going through my training, Philip would take the time to come out to the little airport in Vernon and watch me land on that short runway at the end of my lesson. He even allowed me to fly as pilot-in-command in his own straight-tail Bonanza, which was a much bigger craft than the one I was training in. One such time, I was coming in quite low over a house at the end of the runway and almost hooked the lady's clothesline. The woman whose wash I had almost flown off with as a flying banner called the owner of the airport to complain, and Philip and I had a good laugh about my flying skills.

After about forty hours of training, I was finally sent off on my own to do one solo circuit. While this was a real accomplishment, I never really enjoyed flying enough to be able to call it a passion. However, it made me happy when Philip told me how proud he was of me for becoming a pilot, which gave us another level of safety should he become incapacitated during one of our many flights.

An important part of the training involved practicing recovering from stalls and spins. Although I didn't really care for either manoeuvre, the reason for practicing these skills became apparent one ice-cold Sunday morning. We wanted to go on our usual weekend flight for breakfast in Oliver, BC, which is located just south of where we lived in Kelowna. This was one of our coldest winters ever—the temperature was forty degrees below zero—so the plane had been stored in a warm hangar. We pulled it out and did our walk-around, checking for loose bits and testing for water in the fuel line. Everything looked good, so we climbed on board, got clearance from the tower, and flew off.

We were still climbing at about seven hundred feet when a sudden hush fell over the cabin, leaving only the soft sound of the air passing by the cockpit as the propeller slowed to a lazy turn. The engine had quit! I turned to Philip, white-knuckled and scared, and I could tell that he was concerned too. I quietly grabbed onto the edge of my seat and thought to myself, *If we are going to crash, I will not go down screaming. I will die with dignity.*

Philip had to make a split-second decision. Should he try to belly the plane onto the frozen lake about half a mile from the end of the runway, or should he turn around and glide the plane back to the airport? Deciding on the runway, he put the plane into a slow left bank and radioed the tower to inform them of our situation. The turn had to be very gentle so we wouldn't lose too much altitude—we needed to reach the end of the runway before we could try to land again.

As we approached the airport, everything seemed to unfold in slow motion. We floated toward the ground as emergency vehicles raced alongside us on the taxiway, ready to assist. I could clearly see the faces of the paramedics. Then, just as Philip was about to set the plane down, the engine sprang to life. He had to make some quick adjustments to counter the power surge and avert a potential disaster, but moments later we were finally safely down. We later determined that an ice plug had formed in the fuel line during our climb. Fuel starvation had almost done us in, but with focus and determination we were able to make a successful landing. Philip was truly my knight in shining armour that day!

On top of our love of adventure, we were also brought

together by our interest in helping others. Philip was loved by his patients and was incredibly compassionate. I recall one instance where I saw a two-thousand-dollar charge on his credit card to a pharmacy in the UK. When I asked him about this charge, he confessed that one of his patients needed a medication that was not available in Canada, so he had ordered it for them and would pay for it himself. Similarly, I did everything I could at the bank to help people get into their first homes, including working with an acquaintance in a law firm who would shave his fee to help my customers qualify for their mortgage. Philip and I were both always doing what we could to better the lives of others.

The pursuit of adventure brought many exciting hobbies into our lives, including flying, scuba diving, golf, fishing, and skiing. However, it was our love of helping others that would take us down an incredible path—albeit a very rocky one.

FOUR

Husband Number Two

During the years when Philip was in and out of his marital home, I used the copious amounts of time I spent waiting for him to improve my own home. I added a two-car garage that Philip could hide his car in, as he did not want people knowing he was living with someone else. I did all the landscaping myself to clean up the look of the garden area, planting cedars around the whole perimeter and moving a truckload of bark mulch manually by the wheelbarrow load. And in 1988, Philip gave me what he jokingly referred to as an "engagement pool"—we had a good laugh, but it made me feel that a closer relationship was not far off the horizon. After years of secrecy, I had hopes that marriage might be the next step to being able to live a normal life. I wanted to be able to quit telling lies or half-truths to my family and friends about the man in my life.

However, shortly after moving in with me Philip found an enormous house on the other side of Okanagan Lake that he insisted we buy—I guess he felt that my modest little house, which by now was really a gem, did not adequately reflect his stature in life. The new place was roughly eight thousand square feet spread over three floors with a layout so confusing that I kept getting turned around when we first inspected the house. The top floor contained a kitchen, living room, two bedrooms, one bathroom, a powder room, and another room I came to call the reading room as it eventually contained all our favourite books as well as his medical journals. The next floor down only had a kitchen island in the middle of the room and not much else; it was still in a rough, unfinished state. The basement area, or ground floor, had one huge unfinished room with a twenty-foot-high ceiling that we were told had been a squash court, two potential bedrooms, a bathroom of sorts, and a furnace room. Under the two-car garage was a little one-bedroom suite that needed some TLC, and the yard on the lake side of the house had never seen a gardener's touch. There was also a completely self-contained two-thousand-square-foot suite on the middle and lower level of the north side of the house overlooking the lake. The whole place needed a lot of work and was a huge financial commitment requiring me to sell my house that I loved so much, but I wanted to make Philip happy. This is one of the times I could have made a different choice.

Philip and I got married in April 1991. The wedding was a big secret as he did not want anyone to know—I don't think he wanted people to be aware that he had gotten divorced. I had a marriage commissioner come to the house, and some friends who were now renting rooms in our monstrous house served as the witnesses. The whole thing was over in a matter of minutes. Even my parents didn't know until we took them for a Mother's Day brunch a couple of weeks later and made the announcement. I am sure my mom was hurt and disappointed that she was not a part of the wedding, but she was probably also relieved that I was not "living in sin" anymore. Personally, I didn't mind this low-key event; I was just happy that we were finally married and I was no longer the other woman.

Shortly after we had moved into our new home, we asked my parents if they would like to move into the separate suite.

Their friends advised against it, saying that moving in with your family never works out, but for my parents it was a good decision as I would be able to help them as much as they helped me. So, they moved in, and having this time with them was lovely. Even though they were aging, they still found ways to make my life easier by helping look after the huge house and gardens, and I was able to look after them in their retirement years. Mom and Dad always kept busy—Dad in his little workshop, Mom in the kitchen—and they did not interfere in our lives just as we did not interfere in theirs.

The few people who knew about our relationship envied my position as a doctor's wife, but they didn't know that it wasn't always unicorns and rainbows—that things were not always as they appeared, and to be careful what you wished for. Philip had become quite offhand and distant over the years, leaving me feeling insecure about our relationship. I erroneously thought that getting married would make things better—that he would change and become the man he was when we first started dating. Unfortunately, things only got worse.

Once he got the house he wanted, Philip began chipping away at my self-worth and confidence. His tone was always critical when he spoke to me, although I could never understand why. I constantly had to acknowledge his work ethic and be understanding of how tired he was due to the load he carried at work. I don't know whether he kept so busy because he wanted to be available to his patients or because he was running away from something only he could understand. That being said, he always had time with and for others when he wanted something. He consistently showed a lack of respect toward me, both at home and in front of his colleagues. I felt that I was just a live-in maid, bookkeeper, errand runner, office helper, hairdresser, hostess, and whatever else made his life easier. He continued to lie to others about the fact he was living with me and convinced me to do the same; my friends and family only knew I was living with a man named "Tony" (Anthony was his middle name). I questioned his love for me, but not mine for him.

In retrospect, I can see many similarities between both of my husbands. Both were from the UK. Both had parents who had lost their first born—David lost his sister, Margaret, to a medical error at birth, and Philip's brother, Barry, died in a tragic accident when he was just six, before Philip was born. I now wonder if these tragic deaths hadn't somehow helped create and shape their behaviour.

My relationship with Philip deteriorated to the point where I entertained selling the house and finding another place to live—one where I could take my parents with me. I felt like I was responsible for them now that they had sold their own home to move into ours. However, when I looked around at available properties I quickly realized there were no affordable options that would meet our needs. And truth be told, not so much time had passed since Philip and I had gotten married, and I still had a desire to continue to try and make things work. To me, acknowledging defeat in this relationship represented an even greater failure than the dissolution of my first marriage. How could I admit to anyone that I was once again a victim of emotional abuse? Am I part of the problem?

I started writing Philip emails to let him know how I felt, as he always seemed to respond better to seeing things in writing—he couldn't ignore the black-and-white statements I would make, and he would have time to digest my thoughts and feelings before responding. In retrospect, those emails probably fed my own misery because nothing ever changed. I kept writing them, though, as I hoped they would help him understand my perspective.

After we got married, Philip's spending habits also became a serious cause of concern. I had always known that he was not great with money—after all, I met him when he was applying for a loan—but once we were living together it was impossible for him to hide the true extent of his spending. Various cars that he intended to restore began appearing at our house, and I later learned that several of his patients were storing additional cars on their properties. He would purchase airplanes to partake in his love of flying and because they gave him another means of being able to be somewhere else quickly and easily. He also exchanged perfectly good cars that he drove on a regular basis to get the next biggest and best thing on the market. His income was never enough to cover everything he wanted to buy, so he would borrow to get what he wanted.

When my parents moved into our suite, Philip knew they now had a savings account with a good sum of money in it from the sale of their previous home. He convinced me to ask them for all the money so he could carry on building his little empire of stuff. He promised he would pay it back shortly from the sale of his previous marital home. I was already distrustful of his ability to handle money, so I secretly went and got an insurance policy on my life for the amount he had borrowed and made my parents the beneficiaries—I absolutely did not want to see them lose their life's savings. When the time came to pay the money back, he wanted to renege on paying them the full amount at once and instead arrange monthly payments. I held firm, though, and I made him pay back the loan in full. I wasn't taking any chances.

I would have had no problem with Philip's spending habits if he would have simply set a budget. There was never any money set aside for a rainy day, and we would have been in financial trouble if we lost his income even for a short while.

My income already went fully towards our household expenses, and I did not earn enough to maintain our enormous house on my own. But because I questioned all his spending, I was told I was not being supportive.

It got to the point where he stopped paying his income tax because he was increasing his debt load and had to pay alimony to his ex-wife, even though she was fully capable of working. That was the final straw. To get back to square one financially, Philip declared bankruptcy. Thankfully I was not part of this, so we did not lose the house as it had always been in my name—this was something I had insisted on because it was my money that had made it possible to buy it. I thank God that I'd had the foresight to do that as his spending could have made my parents homeless, and it would have been my fault for getting them into this.

Next came the lying. Women have an intuition that tells them when something is not right, and if you are wise, you will pay attention and listen to it. I had known from the beginning that Philip was not truthful with me on so many levels, but I had hoped that I would be the one for whom he would change. However, as he said so many times to me about others, "leopards don't change their spots."

Sometimes the lies were blatant falsehoods; sometimes, he lied by withholding relevant information that I should have been privy to as his partner in life. He would say he was working late, as he didn't want to come home during rush hour, but that just gave him time to do other things without being questioned. One day, Philip said he had to go to a doctor's retreat for a weekend and would not be allowed to even have his cell phone with him, so I shouldn't expect to hear from him. He did sneak in a call even though he was supposed to be without his phone, so I should have clued in to the lie then.

Later I found out he took someone I knew, another woman, on a fishing trip. This nonsense happened on a regular basis.

As much as I knew Philip was lying to me, it was hard to call him out on it as he would talk in such a way as to make me doubt the original conversation. He would say something to me in anger, then quickly change to a gentler and calmer tone and deny that he had ever spoken differently. He would accuse me of deliberately trying to hear everything he said in a negative way. He would avoid mentioning the specific details of a given situation; if confronted, he would try to convince me that he had told me. He often said things to steer me away from what was going on behind the scenes, and when I questioned him on things I had heard, he would accuse me of having trust issues.

There is a common premise that says if a frog is put suddenly into boiling water it will jump out, but if the frog is put in tepid water which is then slowly brought to a boil, it will be cooked to death. I did not realize that I had become the frog—that the heat was slowly being turned up, and that without me knowing it, I was losing who I had once been.

Philip's emotional abuse turned me around and made me believe that I was the one with the problem. I thought I was lucky to be married to such an accomplished person, and it was hard to believe that the man I trusted and loved could do this to me. I felt like I wasn't enough, and that I wasn't living up to his expectations of me. I had become so unsure of what was real, and Philip seemed to be the one who had things together—a perception he created by gaslighting me. The dictionary definition of gaslighting is "to manipulate (someone) by psychological means into questioning their own sanity." It is a tactic used by abusers to keep their victim off balance by convincing them that certain things were or never were said. Gaslighting can beat you down and make you think you are losing your mind; I didn't think I was going insane, but as the years went on, I did start questioning myself and my recollection of what had been said or not said.

Because I was in denial of what was happening, the dynamic kept going. Philip made up very convincing lies to deliberately upset me. He called me names, then mocked me for getting upset and claimed I was overreacting. He made light of anything that I felt was important and implied that my opinions, life choices, and thoughts were juvenile and inferior to his. My self-esteem and self-confidence were slowly being eroded, and there were many days where there was no joy in my life. I became so insecure that I didn't feel like I could trust my own judgement. Whenever a decision was required, I felt that whatever choice I made would be the wrong one.

I believe the main reason for Philip's gaslighting was to create a dynamic where he had complete control, which made it easy for him to manipulate me so that he could get what he wanted. Looking back now, I can see that it all started with the purchase of our marital home—the one I had to sell my own cute little house for. He made me feel that it would be unreasonable for me to withhold the funds that I would get by selling my house, and I gave in because I loved him.

As bad as this all sounds, I truly believed that everything wrong in our marriage was fixable, although I knew it would take both of us to make the necessary changes. My desire was simple: I just wanted to feel cherished and have balance in my life. I wanted to have a partner I could count on. I wanted him to validate my worth, and I didn't want to depend on outsiders to make me feel valued. Today I know that only I can create my own self-worth, but I still had a long road ahead of me to get to this realization.

After a few years of this toxic dance, I was in a constant

state of bewilderment and confusion. I found it difficult to trust my own mind and constantly doubted my thought process. I always wondered if I was overly sensitive or overreacting. I felt isolated and became reclusive; I felt safer when I didn't have to explain to people what was wrong or what was happening in my relationship.

I was lonely and felt disconnected most of the time. And, having been a child abuse and relationship violence presenter for the Red Cross at local high schools, I knew that I was being emotionally abused. I did not want to continue living like this, so once again I began looking at my options. I sought the counsel of the lawyer who had handled my divorce from David, but he said he was not prepared to act on my behalf as Philip was too powerful in the community—doing so could affect his relationships within the medical community as a conflict of interest. He did, however, refer me to a female lawyer who specialized in divorce matters, and he made an appointment for me to see her that day. I told her about the ways in which he was verbally and emotionally abusing me, and that the marriage was not a happy one. All I got from her was that I couldn't hope to get a good settlement after such a short time, and with all his debt there wasn't much other than our house anyway. I went home and never told Philip what I had done; there was no point.

I kept trying to convince Philip to work on our relationship, and after many notes and emails he finally said, "I think we can and should sort this out. We have too much invested to throw it all away. I do love you still. My life is no fun either." Unfortunately, nothing further changed, and our life together remained a status quo. We continued to live in a civilized limbo with good and bad days, as with any other couple. I went to work each day and participated in team sports to keep in touch with the world. I needed to feel valued, even if it was not from my husband.

You may be wondering at this point why I stuck with him. While our relationship had many challenges, I still loved Philip and admired him in many ways. There was no denying that he was a brilliant doctor—one who had the potential to change the world. And while there were many negative aspects of our life together, the next phase of our lives would bring our greatest contribution to the world: our company, SomaLife, and its patented Youth Formula.

FIVE

Philip – The Early Years

Before I get into how SomaLife came to be and my hopes of a better future, I need to share a bit more about Philip and his medical background.

Born and raised in Bristol, England, Philip knew from an early age that he wanted to become a doctor. He was an excellent student and was chosen to receive a medical scholarship at the Britannia Royal Naval College, one of the most prestigious naval colleges in the world. He conveyed to me that he had accepted their offer, but on further consideration he felt that naval people would be in "such fantastic shape" that they probably would not be much of a challenge for him as a doctor. Philip wanted to make a difference, so initially he went to St. George's, the training hospital in London, and later he chose to attend Cambridge and Harvard University to get his medical degree. He also studied pharmacology and physiology, and he took a special interest in health care economics as well as medical administration. After getting his start in internal medicine (focusing on research for cell repair and regeneration, the body's natural healing factors, and aging and longevity), he decided he would achieve a wider field of treatment by switching to family medicine. However, he never lost his scientific mind and his desire to learn. He was appointed chief of staff and medical director for the Kelowna General Hospital in 1983, a position he held for eighteen years, and it was during this time that he discovered he was in a unique position to take mankind one giant leap forward.

Philip recognized that the majority of money spent on healthcare was in treating the elderly for age-related problems, and that this strain on the system was only going to increase in the coming years. The baby boom that came just after the Second World War started in 1946, and it wasn't difficult to see that this huge bulge in society was just about to hit the high-maintenance stage of their lives and wreak havoc on the medical system. As Philip thought about how to prepare for this situation, he came to a realization: if age-related diseases were the problem, why not stop, or at least slow, the aging process? This may sound like a simplistic reasoning, but for a doctor it was a big jump. He had been trained all his life to treat symptoms, not to solve the underlying problems. It took a man with great foresight to understand that prevention was the key.

At this time, anti-aging was in its infancy. It is always risky to be one of the first to cover new ground, especially with a topic such as this one—many people consider this pursuit to be foolish, with the end goal being an impossible dream. Ignoring this, Philip started delving into the myriad of volumes available on the subject while still maintaining his position as chief of staff and his work as a family doctor. Eventually, he found a possible answer to his search: human growth hormone, or HGH.

For decades, the benefits of HGH therapy have been extremely well-documented. From the discovery of HGH in the 1920s to its first use in growth-stunted children in the late 1950s, the development of synthetic HGH in the 1980s, and its popularity in Hollywood to retain a youthful appearance, we have put a lot of time, effort, and research into its usefulness. It has been long understood that HGH is produced in the anterior pituitary gland, and that after we reach the age of twenty-five, our body—in all its wisdom—decides that we don't need as much as we did when we were younger. This is the start of the aging process. By the time you reach the age of thirty-five, your body produces about two-thirds of the hormone it produced at its peak. By age fifty this is further reduced to around fifty percent, and by age sixty-five we are down to about twenty-five percent. As HGH levels decrease, cell damage increases. In order to slow down this decline, something was needed to encourage the body to continue its natural production of HGH long after nature elected to let us start aging.

One study that showed the benefits of HGH arrived in 1990. Dr. Daniel Rudman received national attention as the principal author of a paper in The New England Journal of Medicine, "Effects of Human Growth Hormone in Men over 60 Years Old." The study was based on a clinical trial of twenty-one healthy men aged sixty-one to eight-one and found that after six months of injections of a genetically-engineered version of the natural human growth hormone, the men emerged with bodies that were—by many measures—almost twenty years younger than the ones they started with. However, Dr. Rudman made it clear that while these results were promising, his methods still needed improvement. "This is not a fountain of youth," he cautioned at the time. "We need to emphasize that the aging process is very complicated and has many aspects." Because his studies were based on the use of injections, he and other experts warned that the dosage of the hormone had to be very carefully calculated due to the possibility of adverse side effects.

Philip did some of his own research, but it wasn't until

1996 that things really kicked into high gear. I was now forty-eight years old and noticing the early effects of aging, and I felt I needed a little help to slow the progression. One night, I asked Philip if he, as a medical doctor and scientist, could come up with something to accomplish this—I knew his ego would drive him to accept the challenge. He told me he thought he might be able to develop something that would be safe, so I said "let's do this" and just left it out there.

Sadly, personal tragedy struck that same year. Philip's brother-in-law, Tony—whom he had a close relationship with—was diagnosed with advanced prostate cancer at the age of fifty-six. He received the standard treatment for the disease, but he continued to deteriorate as the months went on. Finally, he was given six weeks or less to live. Philip wasn't one to just give up, though, and Tony agreed to try some experimental procedures. The two of them headed off to the BC Cancer Agency in Vancouver where several new procedures were being tested, including a carotenoid called lycopene as well as a highly experimental gene therapy. With the introduction of these treatments, Tony's health began to improve and continued to do so for a year—substantially longer than the six weeks allotted by traditional physicians. Unfortunately, there was not a happy ending to this story. Tony didn't die of his cancer; he died from kidney failure. His treatment was so effective that his overloaded kidneys lacked the ability to process the debris from his healing cancer cells. It was the epitome of irony.

Tony left behind three sons, and Philip wondered if there was anything he could do to prevent his nephews from meeting the same fate. Tony's death also reinvigorated my love for helping others. Knowing that Philip was the person with the best chance to do something about this, I asked him, "With all of your years of medical and scientific research, could you create a product to help people live healthier and longer lives?"

Once again, Philip became my knight in shining armour. Spurred on by these thoughts, Philip moved his research into genetics and renewed his interest in age-related disease. He envisioned a society that had virtually won the fight against aging—one where people could live productive and rewarding lives to the age of 120 years or more. He opened the first International Health and Longevity Centre and gathered a team of knowledgeable professionals to staff it. Their laboratory was unceasing in its quest for an effective, safe, and affordable anti-aging product, and they returned to the concept of HGH therapy.

In the past, this therapy was performed by injecting hormones—at first extracted from cadavers and then later synthesized—to artificially raise HGH levels. This is a costly and challenging process, resulting in a treatment that ran into the thousands of dollars per month. Research performed at the International Health and Longevity Centre found that growth hormone did not have to be injected into the body. Instead, we can stimulate our bodies to continually produce more youthful levels of HGH through the use of orally-ingested growth hormone releasers. Because this method does not bypass any naturally occurring processes, the body is able to monitor itself, and a doctor's constant care and supervision is not required, as it is for the injections.

Philip completed his own research into the particular types and amounts of amino acids required to stimulate optimum HGH production in the body. Once he had found the best combination, he had to find a way to manufacture them. Amino acids are derived from proteins, and the type of protein does not affect the quality of the amino acids. So, it made economic sense for us to choose something of reasonable cost—we wanted to do everything we could to keep our product as affordable as possible. We eventually settled on using bacterial fermentation to manufacture our amino acid formula, which was a pure, free-form crystalline amino acid. And with that, our Youth Formula was born!

A good friend of ours had an excellent analogy, dubbed "the Montgomery Elevator Ride," that I find helpful for explaining the benefits of this amazing product. It likens our lifespan to taking a trip in an elevator. At birth, we get on the elevator and begin our ascent toward the top. This is the stage where we are growing, developing, and maturing. We are headed toward the peak of our existence and will soon be at our prime—the time when the elevator has reached the top floor. We'd like to stay there for as long as possible, of course, but the elevator does not stay at the top for long. It soon begins its descent, which represents the decline in our health and fitness that begins around the age of twenty-five. The further down we get, the more we age. Eventually, at the bottom—or perhaps six feet under—the elevator lets us out and our journey is over.

Youth Formula is designed to act like a brake on the elevator. If you can slow down the descent, you will take longer to get to the bottom. You also get to spend more time at the higher floors, so you will stay closer to your peak health for a longer period of time.

All that being said, there is more to staying youthful than just HGH. Philip had six tenets of good health: nutrition, vitamins/supplements, exercise, lifestyle, genetics, and a positive mental attitude. He was sure that a combination of these factors is what would allow a person to achieve both health and longevity—one is no good without the other. What difference would it make for you to live to 120 years if your health had failed and you weren't cognitively aware of what was happening around you?

After the voluminous research he had done and the enormous amount of time he had put into this product's development, Philip needed to protect his creation. So, he got worldwide patents on the formula—an expensive and time-consuming process. Philip had to do the research, create the product, test it in the lab, and provide all the previous studies as well as his own findings to the patent office. I was the first test subject. I would go to the lab and have blood drawn before and after taking the six capsules to show that the product did what we said it did. I immediately felt more energy and was able to do many strenuous tasks with quicker recovery. I slept better, my nails became stronger, and my hair grew quicker. I did not need the blood tests to tell me that my body was getting the wonderful benefits of full body cell repair—I could see and feel the results for myself.

By July 1998, we were finally ready to release our Youth Formula, and our mission to change the world had truly begun.

SIX

SomaLife Is Born

Having a product is one thing, but marketing and selling it is another. Philip, with his commitments to his medical practice, did not have the luxury of time to be hands-on in this process, so it was up to me to determine the setup and operation of the business. I was more than happy to take this on; I had just turned fifty and had recently retired after twenty-five years in the banking world, so this gave me purpose and filled my life. Having been the guinea pig, I knew the product worked, and I was excited to finally have a project with Philip in which I felt I could be in charge. There was also part of me that thought this business would help bring our relationship back to what it was like in the beginning, when we felt we had so much in common and, yes, had a lot of fun.

In the winter of 1998, I began putting everything into motion. We had lots of room available in the house, so I set up an office in the middle floor. I acquired a couple of used desks and filing cabinets, and I had a big commercial printer delivered so we could make our own brochures. We got a dubbing machine and made our own informational cassettes. I bought a ten-foot-long foldable table that we would process orders on. We planned to sell directly to our customers and to use network marketing to get the word out; you cannot simply plop a bottle on a store shelf and expect people to know what it was. I ended up with lots of time to get everything organized as it took almost twelve weeks to receive our first order, and then sales slowly grew organically, through word of mouth, due to the results people were seeing.

Up until now we had done everything by hand, but as things picked up we needed a way to process our orders and commissions more efficiently. I flew to Salt Lake City and purchased a computer program that would run our customer list, maintain inventory records, and calculate commissions. I spent a couple of days there learning how to use the program before flying back home, and when I arrived I learned that Philip had named one of his patients as the director of marketing and put him in charge of ordering our inventory. He had even less qualifications for running a business than I did, but I wanted to build our company and was game to try something new.

Even with this new hire, I was essentially single-handedly getting the company off the ground—setting up accounts with our customers, getting credit card processing in place, and so much more. Thank goodness for my background in banking, which made these tasks relatively painless.

By April of 1999, I hired our first customer service rep, Marlane, as I could no longer answer phones as well as process orders, run commissions, and deal with local customers coming to visit us at the house. Of course, she was another of Philip's patients, but she was willing to do the work and became a very loyal employee. I enjoyed having her around, especially on the days when inventory arrived. A large truck would drop two or three pallets of supplements, packaged in boxes, at the top of an outside staircase that lead to the office on the second level of the house. To move all those individual cartons, each about the size of two shoe boxes, I got a couple of long, two-by-six boards that had to span thirteen steps top to bottom. I then stood at the top and slid the boxes one at a time down the slope to Marlane, who would then carry them into the office. Some of them were stored there, but most had to be carried even further down to a storage room in the ground floor basement. It was a low-tech solution, and we giggled a lot as we shot boxes down this ramp, hoping none of our customers would come by and see us.

Philip had many professional relationships in our community, and he called on them to invest in this new company. A board of directors was created—comprised of local businessmen, other doctors, and even a lawyer—and we had a meeting to decide on a name for the company. Initially the company was called Somatrope Distributing Ltd and the product was called Somatrope, a variation on the name of the growth hormone, somatotropin, produced by the pituitary gland. Some thought this name was too medical and not user friendly for our prospective customers, so in 2000 Philip came up with the name SomaLife for the company—"soma" means "body" in Greek, so the name means "body of life"—and Somatrope became Youth Formula.

After the company was renamed, I created the logo, which is still in use to this day. I drew a circle representing the circle of life, and then an "S" inside the circle to represent SomaLife. The placement of the "S" over the circle created two hearts, one right side up and the other inverted—two hearts had created SomaLife, so to me this was pure magic. Finally, I added a small maple leaf at the tip of the "S" to indicate we were a Canadian company. I later learned that people often paid thousands of dollars to have their company logo created while mine just came to me in a flash of what I now consider brilliance.

Soon we outgrew the office and storage space in the house, so it became time to look for a more official location. The lower floor of Philip's medical building happened to be available, so we did some minor renovations and moved in. This was certainly more convenient for Philip and allowed him to have a physical presence in the company. However, he was intelligent enough to recognize his limitations and set out to engage some business partners. He wanted people who would take the little piggy to market while he stayed home and continued to do what he did best: work to better the lot of mankind and extend the human lifespan even further. I resented that he wanted to hire others who had no skin in the game and no personal interest, but the self-doubt he had instilled in me over the years allowed him to convince me that this was for the best. I later learned that my intuition was right.

We hired our first CEO in 1999. He used to run a company that supplied drinking water and whose wife apparently knew almost as much about hormones and medicine as Philip did—or so he claimed. I'm not sure why that qualified him to be hired to run our company. When Philip was not available, this CEO would bring his wife to company functions and present her as an expert to promote the company and its products. She was beautiful and sounded very knowledgeable, so everyone thought she was great. I, on the other hand, did not like or appreciate that she was taking the accolades for Philip's hard work. This CEO had style but absolutely no substance; he had no regular hours and did not seem to report to anyone. He would float into the office for a couple of hours here and there during each week, but there were never any visible results showing company growth.

One day, he came to me and said he should have double his salary, and that it had been approved. I never thought to double check with anyone as I had no reason to doubt him. I also felt that since he was the CEO, I now reported to him, and no one had made me feel otherwise. This was another time when the insecurity Philip instilled in me perhaps played a role in my decision making; since then, I have learned to trust but also to verify. I generated his next paycheck for the increased amount, and it quickly came out that he had lied. Philip wasn't happy about this, and neither was I, but it was too late to take it back. I also wasn't happy that the CEO was elevating his wife to Philip's level, so I started convincing Philip to fire him. Eventually we got rid of him, but it cost the company two more months of his recently inflated income.

Next, I approached the people who had already tried the product—our "SomaLife family"—to promote the company, and their involvement quickly became a grassroots movement. However, Philip and the board continued to bring on a series of professionals to build the brand, claiming that we needed someone to market and manage the company, and it seemed that anyone we brought in had their own agenda for how our funds should be utilized. I still felt that hiring outsiders was the wrong direction, but I never once thought of taking on a bigger role. I felt that our directors always looked past me as just being the wife of Dr. White, and perhaps they thought that I didn't have the skills to manage anything. As the years passed, all I was asked to do was provide funding to keep the company alive, which I did. This was still my baby—even though it now had foster parents in the guise of outside management—and I was not about to let it die.

The second CEO, who came to us in 2002, claimed that he had been the lead distributor in a well-known multi-level marketing company and had single-handedly brought that company to success. We later found out that he had merely been a regular distributor with another network marketing company, but we all had the wool pulled over our eyes because he was an expert in charisma and charm. We all drank the Kool-Aid. He had SomaLife pay for his vehicle and his gardener. He had us give shares to his father in the UK and then bring him to Canada at our expense to manage our inventory. This CEO stated that his father was the best person for this job, which involved putting little numbered sticky labels on a shelf to show what our products were. We only had five products at the time, which were Youth Formula, an antioxidant, a vitamin, an omega-3 supplement, and a brain health product; a two-year-old could have done this. It was sheer lunacy! He even went on to hire a former coworker of his as an assistant (they had worked together in a factory gassing bananas) and gave her a huge salary in an amount that he said she needed to live on. This was a crazy way to determine a person's wage, but once again we found out too late to do anything about it. She spent a lot of time out of the office due to "family emergencies," and when she was present she just played around on her computer. I'm not even sure why she was hired as I already knew how to do everything in the office—I was the one who had set up all the protocols in the first place—and could have done the work myself. She left shortly after being hired, though, as I had asked her to be accountable and to spend more time at work. She did not like me being the office watchdog. I was the only one who was hands-on with the company and saw how this man was operating, but no one would listen to me about my misgivings. Philip was still caught under his spell and believed that his exuberance would be instrumental in building the company.

The CEO then felt we needed an IT guy. Philip's son, Phil Jr., had been helping me with commissions and server maintenance, but he was not always available due to his work with Interior Health. Many resumes were reviewed with the help of Phil Jr., who recommended we hire Weston. Weston was brilliant with IT and soon he found he didn't have enough work, so he took over some product-related tasks like ensuring our labels were compliant with Health Canada and other regulatory entities. He turned out to be a great hire—this is one of the few things this CEO got right.

The CEO kept hiring more people; I believe he was out of his depth and needed help. Once again, he hired an office assistant—a bubbly blonde who also did not have the qualifications to be of much use, but he loved having his friends around him. Then came an accountant, who was given my office, and I was shunted to another office in a different part of the building. This accountant then promptly hired himself an assistant bookkeeper, and I wondered why no one knew how to do a job on their own. It wasn't like we were like Amazon at the time. Sales were growing, but our expenses seemed to grow right along with them.

Throughout all of this, I did whatever I could to remain a part of the company I had helped create. I was dealing with recurring orders, following up on declined credit cards, and spending time talking with customers, some of whom became friends. However, I could tell the CEO hated me being in the office as I could see what he was up to. Eventually we acquired a new software to run our database, and the company that provided it was based out of Portland, Oregon. The CEO flew down to meet with the owner of the company and made arrangements to lease an apartment nearby, but it wasn't for him—it was for me! He had one of the employees of the software company move into the apartment, which SomaLife paid for, and then he would send me out to these shared accommodations every few weeks to learn how to process commissions. It bothered me to waste all that company money on travel when everything could have been done over the phone or online, but we had put this CEO in charge and had to follow what he thought was best. As I was now working on commission payouts at the end of each month, I was told I had to report to the owner's daughter in that company instead of to the CEO; this was a strategy to keep me out of his way. Maybe this made the CEO happy, but certainly not me!

The final straw came when I discovered that he was having our lead distributors essentially run the company through him, to his and their benefit. He leaned heavily on them for guidance on how to run the company. He would also play favourites with some of the key players and start shifting downlines, which gave them more in commission income. This took commissions away from others, and the people who were losing money were not happy. I also was not happy as this whole process was not transparent and left us open to possible legal action. To me, what was happening was fraud. At this point, I'd had enough. After a lot of complaining I finally got all the directors on board and he was let go.

Many years later, I went to a Direct Sellers Association seminar weekend in San Antonio, Texas. During a conversation with one of the other attendees, I discovered that this last CEO had told others in the Multi Level Marketing world that he had owned SomaLife and had sold it. Thankfully I was able to clear up this lie in the classiest way possible, but this said a lot about his character, and I was vindicated in my feelings towards him.

Because Philip could not promote or endorse our own products, he felt he needed someone other than just himself to support the company by giving seminars on health and healthy choices. While attending an anti-aging event in Vegas, I ran across a woman, Christine, whose husband was a medical doctor in a town about an hour's drive away. I told her what we were doing, and she thought her husband would be open to supporting Philip in SomaLife. He became one of the speakers at SomaLife events and even started writing books on antioxidants and men's health with Philip. The two doctors always put on a very informative presentation and gave a great deal of credibility to what SomaLife offered. Christine and her husband drove to Kelowna on a regular basis, and soon we were fast friends.

Given our good relationship and mutual interests, when one of the many CEOs was let go, Christine stepped in as president of the company while one of our shareholders/directors became the CEO. I was overlooked once again! These two people were to head up the company and work with the board to make all the important decisions. This was all very well until I went into the office one day and found that the large whiteboard in Christine's office had been tagged with "SomaQueen." I was really hurt by this as I had put so much time and effort into the company in so many ways, and yet here was someone who came to the office once a week being called SomaQueen. I also noticed that she was always out of the office, generally going for extended lunches, and that she was doing a lot of texting even during office meetings. Something must have twigged for Christine's husband as not long after, he followed her to Kelowna one week to find she was doing more than just spending time at SomaLife—that she was using these trips to be unfaithful. He came to our house all shaken up and distraught, which caused a great deal of discomfort for all of us, and the relationship between the doctors came to an end shortly after. The sad thing is that our distributors thought Philip and I were to blame for this severed relationship, and we couldn't do anything to correct this misconception as we couldn't tell anyone the truth—it was not our story to tell.

Around this time, the accountant also became a burr under my saddle. He was trying to find a way to get me out of the company, just as the previous CEO had done. I had a feeling he felt threatened by me as I had done a lot of the bookkeeping in the past and questioned why he would need to have an assistant. One day, he thought he had found the excuse he needed. When I had first established the company, we needed to have a credit card merchant provider to process incoming payments for sales. As SomaLife was new, I used an existing but inactive company we had, White Holdings Kelowna Ltd., to qualify for this service as that company had a good credit rating. I attached the merchant account to SomaLife's bank accounts, which was where each deposit would go—all of this was totally transparent. Without consulting with me, the accountant cancelled this service so we could no longer accept Amex payments, and he was intending to go on cancelling the other cards. I believe he thought I was funneling the funds into our personal accounts; he did not realize he would be stopping funds from being deposited to SomaLife. I told him what I thought about his actions and quickly reversed what he had done, and like a kid in grade school, he tattled on me to the CEO. I don't know what he said, but I was soon asked to go for coffee with the CEO and was told that if I wasn't married to Philip, he would have fired me.

I was shocked and angered by this assertion. Here I was, trying to save the company from incompetence and ignorance, and I was chastised for something this CEO did not give me the time to explain nor take the time to understand. Finally, he got the full picture, and after a lot of talk in the office the accountant resigned—although I think he should have been fired.

Next came another hire who would become head of

marketing. After meeting him at the initial interview, I did not like him at all! He bragged about how great he was and everything he could do to make our company a resounding success, but I had a gut feeling about him. I begged Philip not to hire him. I told him if he didn't trust my judgement, he should at least introduce this guy to his two sons—that they would see what I saw. Unfortunately, my pleas fell on deaf ears. Initially this man showed his best side to me, but soon his abrasive ways aggravated our distributors and alienated the staff. He had hired an elderly graphics artist to help him with marketing, but after this "artist" spent hundreds of dollars creating banners in terrible brown colours with misspellings like "sucess" and "tommorow," I said to Philip, "Well, he can't spell, and he has now pissed off our distributors and all our staff. What is left?" After some convincing, we let him go.

The next hire was another Englishman who had been living in the USA, referred to us by the head of the Direct Sellers Association as being a good fit for our company. He seemed to have a lot in common with Philip, including a love of cars, and we subsequently moved him and his family to Canada. He was charming with a lovely wife, two great kids, and a dog. They temporarily moved into our home, and I had high hopes that we had finally found someone who could truly take SomaLife to where it needed to be.

At this time the board felt that building our own warehouse rather than leasing would improve our efficiency and company growth, so in 2004 we built a combined warehouse and office building in the industrial area of Kelowna. Now we could have everything in one location and have a suitable place to entertain our visiting distributors. The building was much bigger than we needed, though, and after three years we had not grown to fill it. We found a local construction company that needed a larger building and took over their lease, which suited us better, while they took on ours. These new offices were located above a restaurant and had an outdoor patio upstairs with a lovely view over a park and just a glimpse of the lake. The only downside was that we once again had to set up shipping in another area of town, which meant that not all staff would be in the office at the same time.

We brought in a new accountant who had been referred to us; he quickly settled in and (of course) hired an assistant. Here we go again. He was constantly wasting time and left everything for his assistant to do. He did not even do the year-end accounting to be submitted to Revenue Canada; we paid another accounting firm to do this. Philip got tired of asking him for our current financials, which to this point he had never been able to receive from anyone in the history of SomaLife. I still don't know how one can run a company without proper financial information. Numbers were just being moved around, and even with my years of banking experience I couldn't make sense of most of it. I was asking questions and Philip was frustrated not knowing where we stood financially in the company, and yet we still couldn't get the information we were looking for. This is when the accountant's assistant, whom I had a very good relationship with, confided to me that the CEO had told the rest of the staff to keep me out of accounting. Red flags galore!

Next came the new marketing guru, Glenn, who was to create a new training system for our distributors. He was charming and flattering, and I felt that finally we had hired a winner who would help the CEO move the financial needle in the right direction. Unfortunately, the CEO eventually stopped paying the marketing guru, and he faded off into the sunset.

Despite all of my optimism, things were not getting

better. Around this time, an injection of funds was needed as there was nothing in place to set money aside for replacing inventory before it was needed. Philip went to all of his friends and associates, but no one was willing to lend the one hundred thousand dollars we needed to keep the company afloat. Philip suggested to me that Lena, his office manager, had recently come into a large inheritance and might be willing to assist us; I had misgivings, but in the end I gave in and we set up a loan with her. The terms were very generous in her favour, included shares in the company as well as ten percent interest upfront. The CEO then purchased eighty thousand dollars of a product that did not have a robust sales record, and subsequently much of it expired before it could be sold and had to be destroyed. He made sure he received his salary, but there were several times I had to personally provide money to make sure the rest of our staff got paid on time.

After four years with us, the CEO had to take his family back to the US so his two children could finish their education there. We should have terminated his employment then as you cannot run a company in absentia, but he had assured us it would be possible so we were willing to give it a try. By this time, we were in such bad shape financially that the decision was made to terminate everyone except one customer service representative, the accountant's assistant, the COO, the CEO, and me. I was also asked if I would allow the company to move back into our house; of course, I said yes. In 2010 we set up the whole basement as both office and warehouse; twelve years after we first created SomaLife, we found ourselves back where we had started.

We were still using network marketing at this time and our commissions payout was in excess of fifty-four percent, which was way too high when you factored in all the other costs that came from purchasing inventory, paying the office staff, and covering general expenses. So, we made the decision to close down the network marketing program and change to direct sales through our website. This upset a lot of our distributors who had built reasonably good incomes, but there were also many happy product users who did not care if we paid commissions or not—they just wanted to be able to buy the products.

Unfortunately, our financial issues were about to hit a new level. I got a phone call from the bank informing us that they had been served a garnishee order for fifty-three thousand dollars on the SomaLife account as our in-house accounting department had not been paying GST (a tax imposed by Revenue Canada). This meant that the account was frozen until the debt was paid. I soon learned that they had been sending us numerous letters reminding us to make payment, but no one had been opening the mail—it just sat on top of a file cabinet, unopened, in the bookkeeper's office. She was apologetic and begged me not to tell the CEO, but I had to so that he and I could deal with this disaster. Needless to say, she was terminated immediately. I contacted the government to make arrangements for monthly payments, and in the meantime SomaLife operated out of a US dollar account which the Canada Revenue Agency could not touch. From then on, I made sure I personally opened every piece of mail that arrived, and still do to this day.

Trying to run a Canadian company from California wasn't working, so CEO number five was let go. I was now the only one somewhat in charge—together with the COO, who was also offsite but still in the same town—and over the next two years I slowly got our funds back under control. We were then offered a great deal on a little standalone building on the lake just two minutes from my house, so we accepted and moved once more. I was happy to be back in a proper business location; it had been hard to have business traffic continually coming through our home.

Even though the latest CEO was gone, the COO stepped into his shoes and made the day-to-day decisions while I looked after paying company bills, writing various reports, and managing finances. He had his eyes on being the next CEO, but at this point Philip was reluctant to bestow that title on anyone else—at least for now. There was never any thought of me taking anything over as there was now not much to take over. We also had two customer service representatives and a bookkeeper of sorts, and we were just limping along trying to keep the company viable. I felt beaten down, both in my relationship with Philip as well as in my role with the company. I'd once had a hope, a vision, a dream—where had it gone?

I had to go back and think about why we had started the company in the first place. Youth Formula had helped so many people feel better and maintain their youth, myself included. I could not give up now. We had such heartwarming, amazing testimonials, and I knew I had to continue to fight to keep SomaLife alive.

SEVEN

Everything Changes

While SomaLife was going through this rollercoaster, which occupied much of my time and thought, I was also facing new difficulties in my relationship with Philip. Even with this company offering a new common ground that I had hoped would bring us together, he remained distant and disconnected. And then, in 2007, everything changed—just not the way I wanted.

Philip's sister Valerie was visiting us in Canada when she got news that her son, Addison—who was in his early twenties—had gone missing back in the UK. It was feared by the police that he had committed suicide—or worse, that someone had killed him. This was a heartbreaking time for all of us, especially as there was so much uncertainty. Valerie did not want to share this information with her frail mother, who had come on the trip as well, out of fear of what the news would do to her, so she tried to hide her tears while we sat on the sundeck and talked in whispers. She had already lost Tony, and now she might have lost one of her sons as well.

A few days later, I received an email—perhaps by accident, perhaps on purpose—from Philip's office manager. In that moment, my whole world turned upside down. For whatever reason, my husband had forwarded her my email telling him of Addy's disappearance, but with an appended note to her in which he addressed her as "My dear Lena" and signed off with "Love P XXXXX."

I was shocked. I was hurt. I was devastated. I was angry.

With that email, I finally had proof of the relationship I had suspected for years. Lena was not only his office manager but also, of course, a patient of his. I was in his office the day he hired her, and in my heart of hearts I was not happy with this decision. I knew she had been enamoured with people in medicine—Philip had previously shared with me that she'd had a short-lived affair with a veterinarian. Now, it appeared that she was trying to up her game.

Right from the beginning, it was obvious she was attracted Philip. She was openly possessive of him, to the point that she made me feel uncomfortable with my own husband. I did not like being around her, but she was hard to avoid as she was always present at the various events and functions we attended. I had, on many occasions, jokingly called her his "other wife"; I guess the joke was on me. I had complained to him about her constant presence and told him I thought she had a thing for him, but he had repeatedly brushed me off by saying, "Don't worry, she's not my type." On one occasion, he even told me I was paranoid. Like a fool, I had believed him—I hated confrontation and believing him was just so much easier.

Once again, my intuition was right.

After reading this shocking email, I called Val into the room and showed it to her. She was aghast that he would share this very personal information with his patient/employee, and that Lena had been so vile as to forward it to me. Valerie's heart was breaking with news that her son was missing and feared dead, and here was her brother sharing that information with someone the two of us considered to be an outsider.

The betrayal I was feeling took on a life of its own. I was

so angry that I immediately called Lena's home. Her husband Dale answered, and when I asked to speak to Lena, he said she had moved out two years prior. She had been housesitting for friends until recently, when she had purchased a condo with the inheritance money she had received after her mother's death. Apparently, the condo she purchased was two blocks from Philip's office.

The shock of learning that she no longer lived with her husband just added to my anger and confusion. I didn't even know that Lena and Dale had separated. How could Philip have forgotten to tell me this? I told Dale about the email, and he told me they had been an item for years—that the reason he and Lena had separated was because he had come home and found her and Philip in a compromising position. Dale said he had thought of telling me but never did, although he was surprised that I did not know. I have no idea why he did not tell me, and I truly wish he had. Maybe it is true that the wife is always the last to know.

When Philip came home that afternoon, I had a large picture of Lena displayed on my computer monitor. As soon as he walked in, I said, "You're busted." He looked confused for a moment, then replied, "No I'm not." He was always one to deny, deny, deny.

I told Philip I had called Dale and talked to him about the email, then asked, "Why don't I call Lena and ask her myself?" He seemed dumbfounded. I asked him for her phone number and he claimed he did not know if he could remember it. That was the most ridiculous thing he could have said—I knew that he called her on a regular basis. He was hedging, hoping I would not follow through. After some pressuring, he reluctantly gave me her number—from memory, of course.

Philip was in the room with me when I called her. I accused

her of having an affair with him, asked her how long this had been going on, and demanded to know what she thought she was doing. Her only response was, "I don't know what to say." She asked if he was there with me and I said, "Yes, he is. Would you like to speak to him?" I think that surprised her and told her the game was over—at least, I thought it was. I remember her feebly saying, "I've known him longer than you have," which to me was such an absurd attempt to justify their affair, as well as completely irrelevant.

I asked Philip about her new living arrangements—I wanted to find out if he would tell me the truth. He said that he did not know where her condo was, that he did not get personally involved with his staff. If I had not been so mad, I would have laughed.

I brought the email up again, and he told me the text had been changed. He claimed that someone was out to get him, that he had enemies, and that the original version did not include the offending endearments. He was still in the mode of deny, deny, deny. He followed up by sending me an email to inform me that someone was monitoring Lena's email and playing malicious games. I felt as I were living in a soap opera!

I told Philip he could no longer have her working for him, and that I would email her a termination notice. He seemed to accept this as inevitable, so two days later I did exactly that. I also sent her a personal note telling her that Philip could no longer be her personal physician, and that if anyone asked why she wasn't around anymore, I would tell them that Philip and I both felt uncomfortable with her unwanted advances towards him.

Philip was still trying to convince me the email had been sent to me as part of an evil plot by one of his office staff. A week after my discovery, he came into my office and logged into his email account on my computer. He wanted to show me the "undoctored" version of the email to prove his innocence. Once he thought he had made his point, he left my office; unbeknownst to him, he had not logged off. I checked his sent folder and lo and behold, I found further proof of his relationship with Lena. Enemy in his office, indeed! He had been caught red-handed, and nothing he could say would change that.

As I looked through his sent folder, I found some emails between him and a woman named Hanna. She'd had some dealings with our company in the past as a business consultant and was the sister of the first marketing manager we had hired, so I was curious to find out what they might be emailing each other. And with each message I read, I could feel my heart pounding as the layers of the onion started to peel back. Judging by the dates on the emails, he was playing two women at the same time—one locally in his office, the other one about three hundred miles away in Vancouver. Owning his own plane was very convenient as he could fly there and back without me even knowing he had been out of town. He always kept to a certain schedule, so I never questioned his absence so long as it fell within those expected times.

My imagination went into overdrive. As soon as I really understood the height of their emotional attachment, I sent off an email of my own to Hanna. I told her Philip and I had talked and he had agreed to step away from their relationship. I told her there was no professional or personal reason he would need to further engage with her on *any* level.

I once again confronted Philip and asked him how long this affair had been going on, and he finally said at least five years. I believe it was much longer than that. I asked him why he had kept up a relationship with Hanna, and he replied that it was a "trivial pursuit" and "game playing." He said it was a fantasy he was living, and in the end did not mean anything. I told him it meant something to me, and it had to stop. I said I would be giving Hanna a call, and he responded that he had already proactively called her to warn her of this. He was always good at covering his tracks and likely wanted to coach her on what to say to me.

Once we finished talking, I got up the courage to call Hanna. I told her that I knew what was going on, and that he had another woman on the side. After that, I got a lot more information from her; things like she felt they had an "odd" relationship and that they had a fantasy life. I let her know he wasn't who she thought he was. Hell, he wasn't even who *I* thought he was.

I accused Philip of betraying me and he just kept denying it. Even in the face of such strong evidence of his infidelity, he would not admit what he had done.

After the discovery of these affairs, I was in immense emotional pain and my heart felt so heavy. Unfortunately, I couldn't really talk to anyone else about what was going on. Philip was a well-known doctor in our community, so I was still trying to protect his image—partly because it reflected on me and because I didn't want the embarrassment of people knowing about my unhappiness. Apparently, this was an exercise in futility. As I later learned, Philip had a reputation in our town of being a womanizer as he had not been particularly discrete, which left me looking like a fool.

I needed to understand the motivation behind his actions— the reasons why he behaved like this—and figure out how I could live with his affairs, so I started to search the internet for information on the subject. I eventually found a site that offered support and information for victims of adulterous spouses as well as cheaters looking to better understand their own infidelity. The information I found here helped a lot, and I started to journal about the things I felt I needed to deal with—particularly my feelings of anger and hurt. I needed to vent about whether or not I should try to save our marriage, and I needed the anonymous people on the site to tell me that I was not alone.

I continued to write Philip to tell him the changes we could make to improve our lives and regain much of what we had lost. I gave him the opportunity to make things right if he wanted to; in fact, I gave him a lot of chances. However, should he not want to make things right, I also provided him with a few options:

1. We separate immediately, sell the house and all other assets, and transplant my parents to another home that would work for them. He could then become the recluse he wanted to be with the understanding that he would have a financial responsibility to me so that I could have a reasonable life.

2. Both of us stay in the house but live separately until one of my parents were gone, and then we would conclude matters. I would then need a house that would be shared with my remaining parent; he could keep the behemoth and do what he wanted with it.

3. He moves out of the house, but his financial responsibility to me remains the same.

I didn't include SomaLife in these plans because I truly believed that if any of these options were triggered, the company would cease to exist. I was the glue that held the company together, and it was solely my passion. I had a vision; everyone else had an agenda.

All of these options meant it would be over between

us—that we would live our own separate lives and do whatever with whomever. I assured him that I would not plan to take him to the cleaners as that is not who I am. Even when I separated from my first husband, I just walked away when I could have taken him for half of his retirement savings, and I willingly shared in the loss that came with a lower accepted price on the sale of our house. I had no wish to hurt my partners despite the hurt they had caused me. However, I had invested a lot of time and money into my relationship with Philip, and I expected a fair return of that investment.

During all of this drama, Valerie had gone back to the UK. A body had been found, but they would not know if it was her son's until DNA testing had been done. Shortly after her return, she emailed me to thank me for everything, and to let me know that there was still no real news about Addy. The DNA testing confirmed it was him, but the coroner said that his body could not be released until all questions were answered about some suspicious circumstances surrounding his disappearance and death. The whole situation was inconceivable, and my heart ached for Valerie; selfishly, though, it was difficult to have her leave. She was my greatest support, especially as I had no one else to talk to. I was still keeping all the relationship drama in-house, and I didn't want to talk to my parents either as I didn't want to burden them with worry. I was now anxious all the time and became unable to sleep.

Two weeks after I discovered the affairs, Philip became impatient with my constant questioning and told me to "get over it." After all his years of infidelity, he was giving me two weeks to get over it! In addition, he never responded to a single thing I had written—I guess he thought that if he ignored it long enough, I would forget about it and go on to something else.

I called Hanna again and told her that he had admitted his affairs were just a game and gave her details about his other activities without telling her who the person was. I think she was shocked by this disclosure, but she kept things very civil, as did I. I let her know that Philip was not prepared to lose everything, and that a lot of lives had been affected by his fantasies. I told her I hoped that she could find someone nice to treat her the way she should be treated, because in truth she was a nice person. It surprised me to think of her that way, but I had always liked her, and perhaps I was putting the blame where it belonged. She told me Philip was lucky to have someone who loved him as much as I did.

Hanna asked me how I was going to get through this. I told her that I was stronger than he gave me credit for, and that I would just do it. In the end, we wished each other well. Now that I had clearly told Hanna where I stood, I felt like Philip had lost a lot of mental and emotional power over me. As I would soon find out, he had more power over me than I knew.

EIGHT

Broken Promises

Although I felt I dealt with Hanna and Lena quite well—an assessment my sister-in-law agreed with—I was still trying to comprehend exactly why these affairs happened. When Philip and I got married, our vows explicitly included a promise of "forsaking all others," yet he had broken this promise by forming a strong emotional attachment to at least two other women during our marriage, maybe more. This constituted a breaking of a trust, a bond, that we were supposed to have. Philip said his relationships were fantasies, but once a relationship is grounded in everyday life, the excitement and the idealized image of the partner quickly disappear. Is that what happened with me? The excitement went away? He used to say one had to nurture a relationship to keep it strong. Why didn't he nurture *our* relationship?

I was confused and had so many questions, ones that I'll never get an answer to. He kept walking away from me when I wanted to talk and did not show any remorse that I could discern. He didn't give me any reassurance that he cared about me, not just the lifestyle I helped provide. Instead, he became even more distant, to the point that we were both just operating in our own bubbles. He made several comments along the way that I was nasty, and that people didn't like me; when I asked him who, he could not, or would not, give me an answer. That was part of his game: throwing out hurtful comments that would fester in my psyche and cause me a lot of emotional pain. I was in denial about how he behaved, and that was probably part of the problem. I was an enabler, my inaction giving him permission to continue treating me this way.

Once his affair with Lena was exposed, Philip moved out of our bedroom and set up camp on a different floor of the house. This did not hurt me as much as the denial of his affair did. I was angry at first, and then I just resigned myself to the fact that nothing would change, no matter how much I wanted it to. I had always loved and admired Philip for his brilliance, and even after all that had happened, I still did. However, he was a very complex person, and I was finally accepting the fact that he was not who I thought he was.

At this point I had a decision to make: either I had to find a way to make things work between us, or I had to leave and start over. And while there were many reasons to leave, there were almost as many reasons to stay. For one, keeping SomaLife alive was a passion I could not easily let go. I felt I had a responsibility to the company's shareholders and to the people who had come to depend on the dietary supplements they received from us, and I feared that the company would quickly go under if I left. I was the person who kept it financially afloat when money was short, and I was the one who had the strongest desire to keep it going. Also, many relationships had been forged over the years and customers had become friends, and I did not want to share with any one of them what a disaster our marriage had become. Another consideration was that Philip refused to leave our home, which I had purchased with my life's savings, and I could not walk away from it. And finally, my relationship with Philip had gifted me a wonderful family of two stepsons, their wives, and three grandchildren between them. Outside of my parents, my own family had distanced themselves from me because Philip was married when we first got together, and this distance grew further when Philip wanted nothing to do with my brother and his family. These relationships would be mended later on, but for now Philip's family was all I had and I did not want to give them up.

Philip felt that we could coexist in the house, but it soon became apparent that living in this manner would give him more freedom while making me a prisoner of his choices. Infidelity was not on the menu for me, so I would remain married but alone. Since we both refused to move out, I had no choice but to make the best of what we had.

In order to come to grips with his actions, I did a lot of reading and thinking. I read that serial affairs may indicate an addiction to sex, love, or romance, and that because of their actions, addicts are often consumed with feelings of shame and worthlessness. I often wonder if Philip felt worthless because he was away in medical school when his father died. His father, who had been a submariner during the war, had passed away in his sixties due to a reaction to a dye that had been inserted into his bloodstream for a medical test—he was mowing the lawn one minute, and then Philip's mother saw him collapse as she stood by the kitchen window. Philip often mentioned that if he'd been there, he could have prevented his father's death; perhaps this contributed to his actions.

I also read that attractions are a fact of life when men and women work side by side. Most people can resist such temptations, but I truly believe Philip was hard-wired to cheat—after discovering his affairs in our relationship, I learned that he had liaisons with other women outside of his first marriage as well. It was all about ego and "because he could."

Philip and I would often sit on the balcony of our house,

which overlooked the lake, and this is the setting where I found it easiest to try to get him to open up—to tell me why he needed these other women in his life, why the betrayal. He never had an answer. I asked if he had ever had a "love of his life," and he said yes, a girl by the name of Jennetta back in England. However, he would never tell me why that relationship had floundered. I am a little ashamed having done this, but I found out later by hacking his email that he had tried to reconnect with her during one of our trips to visit his family in the UK. Her response was to decline his offer to meet with him as she did not want to jeopardize her relationship with her husband, Paul. From the gist of her email to Philip, I got the impression he had done something seriously wrong that caused her to bail from this relationship back in their youth. After Jennetta, I don't think he could ever really love anyone in that way again. I think he knew he had made a huge mistake, but who knows where that relationship may have ended given his track record. In the end, I realized that I was just one of many, and it was now clear that all the women in his life were simply pawns for the King.

One concern I kept returning to was that Lena was both his patient and employee. In this scenario, a romantic relationship is problematic at best because there is a serious imbalance of power. In fact, a doctor can lose his license for engaging in an affair with a patient. Yet Philip behaved like the rules of fidelity did not apply to him, and Lena was prepared to live on the fringes with him—at least for a time. Personally, I felt that she should get herself another fantasy to live in. She had destroyed her own marriage; I would continue to fight for mine.

While I truly wanted to work things out with Philip, I was not willing to settle for a relationship in which I was disrespected. I loved him, but I wanted all of him. I wanted total truth and honesty about everything. I decided that if he was willing to renew our marriage vows—to renew his promise of faithfulness and provide genuine assurance that he would not betray me again—then we could perhaps move forward. I also needed him to give me as much time as I needed, not as little time as he did, to get past this.

Unfortunately, things were not moving in the right direction. Despite having sent Lena a termination letter days earlier, I became aware that she was still working in the office. Philip said she had a few things to finish off, but I didn't believe him. After another sleepless night filled with anxiety, I decided I'd had enough. I strongly suspected that these two affairs were just the tip of the iceberg—that there were even more lies, delusions, deceits, and betrayals I had yet to discover—and I just did not see how we could fix things.

When Philip got up that morning, I told him that I wanted a legal separation. He avoided the topic by claiming he had been offered a job in Ireland that paid five thousand pounds per week as they were so short on doctors. He said he would go there and just send me money until there was "a change in circumstances," whatever that meant. As usual, he was not dealing with the issue in front of him.

When I spoke with Valerie about this, she said it was known in the UK that the Irish government had in fact trained too many doctors, and that there weren't enough jobs available for the ones already there. This threat to move to Ireland was just another distraction, and as usual, nothing came of it—it was just more smoke. He always had a way of shifting the focus away from whatever I wanted to talk about.

The whole time I was dealing with Philip's infidelity, Valerie was dealing with her own grief. The coroner had yet to release her son—they were still determining cause of death but were beginning to suspect that it was simply a tragic accident. At this point, she just wanted Addy back so that they could have the funeral and she could bury him next to his father. We emailed each other daily to offer support.

After more than a month of fighting about Lena and her presence at the office, I emailed Philip and implored, "Philip, please make the time *today* to write that closure email to Lena with a CC to me, NOT a BCC. This is important to me. Then, other than you dropping her as a patient, this is over! Please make sure she is aware in that email that you can no longer be her physician, ever."

He responded with, "Will do, but I am not going to put the patient bit in the email as that begs a question and gives potential ammunition. Here is what I intend to send. It keeps everything professional and is what would be anticipated in a normal departure. I will send it with a copy to you:

> "Dear Lena, *further to our recent conversations regarding your office involvement because of your increased workload at school and pursuit of higher education, I am sending this email to confirm our discussions. I realize that you will no longer be able to perform your office duties because of the above and that as requested your last day of tying up loose ends was yesterday, Friday, October 12.*
>
> "I would like to take this opportunity to thank you for all of your hard work over the past several years, particularly with implementing the chronic care modules. The office staff will miss you and your involvement, but we all wish you well in your new endeavors. Sincerely, Philip White."

Philip had written her dismissal letter in a way that sounded like it was her idea to leave, and if that's what it took to get rid of her, I was okay with it. I thought we were finally getting to the end of several weeks of emotional pain and could look forward to rebuilding what we had lost. Unfortunately, there was still more pain to come.

NINE

My Hero Dies

Just as all of the drama with Philip seemed to be settling down, my father—who was in his nineties—began feeling worse after several days of being unable to eat or sleep. Philip went downstairs to their suite to check on him and immediately insisted we call an ambulance and get him to the hospital. Soon two ambulances and a fire truck arrived, and the house was swarmed with about ten firemen and paramedics. Mom went with him in the ambulance, and as Philip and I watched the vehicle slowly drive away, I wondered if I would ever see my father again.

When I went to pick Mom up three hours later, Dad was looking a little better but had what seemed to be millions of tubes sticking out of him. This is the first time he had ever been in a hospital, but he had a big smile on his face and was telling jokes as usual. While his attitude was good, his diagnosis was not. They had discovered he had a lot of fluid in his lungs, severe congestive heart failure, and poor kidney function, so he would likely be in the hospital for at least a week.

A doctor asked me if they should try to resuscitate my dad if it came to that—Mom was too distraught to make any kind of a decision, and the English language was still a bit of a barrier for Dad. As Dr. White's wife, they seemed to expect me to be in charge. That question sure sounded like his condition was serious, especially as I knew he had also been dealing with angina for a long time. Because of his age and the invasive medical treatment that might be used to resuscitate him, I discussed this decision with Philip—I trusted him to help make the right decision in this regard, but not much else. Philip told medical staff to try aggressive treatment first, but if it did not work then do not resuscitate. It sounded so horrible, but I agreed it was for the best. Philip had once told me that the Intensive Care Unit would look like a war zone after a resuscitation attempt, with plastic, paper, gloves, and other medical trash strewn everywhere. The lead doctor and other clinicians would do forceful chest compressions, probably breaking some ribs, and there could be brain damage. I did not want this for my father, and I knew that he would never want to survive a heart attack if it meant he would no longer have any quality of life.

We brought Mom back to an empty house, and while there was a lot of sadness and worry, at least she could have a restful night for a change knowing that my father was in good hands. Dad's inability to sleep had been keeping her awake as well.

The following day, we found out that Dad's condition was much worse than we'd thought. He'd had a massive heart attack at home before he was taken to the hospital. The day after that, they had a mask on him pushing oxygen into his lungs to try to clear them; his kidneys were failing and were not removing the fluid surrounding them. The doctor said the next thirty-six hours would be critical, and Philip said he had a thirty percent chance of making it. Thankfully, by the end of the day Dad had improved and was given a sixty percent chance. I felt sorry for Mom as she hadn't been able to sleep during these days, but then my brother and sister-in-law took her up to the hospital and she looked a little less stressed when she came home. Phil Jr. called me after Philip had told him about my dad, and it meant a lot to me to have him reach out. Both boys were genuinely nice people and were big on family.

On October 25, 2007, a week after Dad went into the hospital, Mom and I were getting ready to go visit him when I got a call from Philip. He said that Dad had done well overnight and was even making jokes with Philip when he looked in during his morning rounds, but a few minutes later his heart had given out and he had died. It was just like Dad to be happy right before he passed—he had been an upbeat kind of guy as long as I'd known him. Unable to process this information, I simply got in the car and left for the hospital with Mom. It wasn't until we were almost halfway there that I finally found the words to tell her that her partner of almost sixty-five years was gone. I think she was in shock at first; the reality of it didn't seem to hit her until we went into his room and saw him for ourselves. He was lying peacefully in bed with one arm below the covers—perhaps covered up by the nursing staff—but he did not look like my dad anymore. His joyful smile was gone. I touched his arm and it was still very warm. He and Mom had worn matching copper health bracelets, and I asked her if I could have his as it would mean a lot to me. She said yes, so I gently removed it from his wrist. This was the only thing I wanted from him.

As I write this, I have tears in my eyes for a man who made a difference. He was a man who moved to a foreign land to make a new home for his family, a real pioneer, and was loved by all who knew him. He was my hero.

The days leading up to the funeral were difficult for all of us. Mom was devastated, and it showed deeply in her face. I took charge of the arrangements so I could be sure Dad would go out in style—his funeral had to be as special as he had been.

We waited until November first as we didn't want to say our final goodbye on Hallowe'en, and it was a perfect day. The men's choir he had been part of for many years sang, and my niece and I each went up front to give a speech. My eulogy was short, but it conveyed what my father meant to me:

> *Dad,*
>
> *Your physical presence may be gone but your spirit will remain forever.*
>
> *Ah, your spirit! There are just not enough words to express the depth of your spirit and what you meant to me. But one word says it all: amazing!*
>
> *Christopher, your grandson, said it so well in his letter to you. You were his hero. You helped a little boy, who is now a man with two little boys of his own, learn from you and figure things out with your love and support.*
>
> *Your love of music and theatre saved your life during the war because you were allowed to entertain the Russians while you were held captive for two years. But you survived that ordeal, which made it possible for me to become your daughter. Thank you for that gift.*
>
> *You were a pioneer in so many ways, bringing your family to Canada in 1954. Without even knowing the language, you took on the challenge of moving to a foreign land. You made a good life for your wife, Emmi, and your three children by working hard and by being a man of strength and integrity. You took great pride in your good name, and you gave us all the opportunity to become the best we could be.*
>
> *You always saw the glass half full, and you always had a smile on your face and a musical instrument nearby. You once said to me, "Do everything you want to do while you are young enough to enjoy yourself. Life is short."*

My brother Udo, my sister Eileen, and I had the honour of having you as our father for ninety-one summers. That is a long time to live but seems very short when you put a number to it. You were right, as usual.

You were a practical man and always looked for ways to make something work better or more efficiently. You were a problem solver, and having you and Mom live in the same house with us the last seventeen years added colour to our lives. You loved to sit in your swing with Mom on a sunny day, enjoying the peace and watching all the wildlife on and around the lake.

You were highly regarded by all who met and got to know you, especially all your friends and their wives in the German men's choir. You played your music, danced, and sang with joy, and you lived.

You were always interested in the many aspects of life and living, and you made the best of the time you were given. Your heart at the end, though tired, was pure.

"Soon another season will pass, and the trees will give birth to a new generation of blossoms. Flowers that grow where old ones have withered serve to remind us that an ending will one day come to us all." —from Memoirs of a Geisha

Dad, you have always been my hero.

Love, Marlies

At the end of the service, I had them play the song "Time to Say Goodbye" by Paul Potts; that song shall always hold a special place in my heart. I was thankful that I was able to find pansies for the floral arrangements as they were his favourite flower. At the cemetery, I put a gold medal I had won for the Top Women's Dragon Boat Racing Team—a sport I had picked up at fifty years old—in the vault next to the urn holding his ashes, along with a copy of my speech. Then there was a tea at the German club, catered by the wives of the men's choir so that Mom and I didn't have to do anything. My dad would have loved every part of it.

Now that Dad had been laid to rest, I returned to dealing with my own personal agony. At least I'd had a little bit of respite from it, although that wasn't pleasant either.

During my research into surviving infidelity, I read that seventy percent of couples who seek help after a full-fledged emotional affair are able to stay together if they sincerely want to—that even if one person had crossed the line, the relationship still has a fighting chance. However, it also said that "surviving infidelity is not about what happened and why, it's about how you respond to it together. You must decide: are we going to let this destroy us, or make us stronger?" Why did this not make me feel better?

The articles I read went on to talk about the positive steps that Philip needed to take—a relationship cannot be fixed if only one person of the couple is making the effort. First, he needed to take responsibility for what he had done. Philip did not screw up because of something I did; he screwed up because he screwed up. He was not doing well in this regard.

Second, Philip needed to offer me a sense of security by giving me what I needed to feel safe. If I wanted him to cut off contact with the other women or asked him to come straight home from work, he needed to say yes and follow through. There was also a lot of room for improvement in this area. Despite Philip's email terminating Lena's employment, she was still working at the office. He kept saying she was tying up finishing up loose ends, but one of his office girls told me that they had all her "loose ends" under control and couldn't understand why she was still coming in. In hindsight, I believe he kept this charade going because he was worried about her reporting their liaison to the college. Regardless, I was sick of all the delays.

Finally, Philip needed to be patient with the rollercoaster of emotions I was experiencing—he had to be a healer in the truest sense. I was cool one day, furious the next. This whole situation was so painful.

I kept in touch with Lena's husband on a casual basis as he was someone I could talk to. Through our conversations, I learned that Philip had inserted himself into this family. He had purchased a very expensive stethoscope for one of Lena's daughters who was thinking about becoming a veterinarian, and he had loaned cars to the other so that she could travel out of the province. I wondered why Philip was acting as the father figure to these girls when Dale was ready and willing to maintain his relationship with them.

I decided to approach Philip about this. However, when I told him I had talked with Dale, he responded that I had just put the last nail in his coffin, and that Dale would likely now report him to the medical college for inappropriate behaviour. I highly doubt that Dale ever would have reported him as I believe that Philip was blackmailing him—he knew that Dale did some work under the table and could have reported him to the Canada Revenue Agency. This seemed to be another attempt to deflect and distract, although this time he went even further than usual.

Philip told me he was not going to live in fear of that happening and then left, saying I would not see or hear from him again. He said that I would have to live with the responsibility of him doing this—whatever "this" turned out to be—and that he knew how to do it so that it would look like natural causes. He also said that doing what I did got me what I had wanted. He later called me from his office and said he was getting his affairs in order so that I would be okay financially. I read all this as him saying goodbye forever—that he was going to take his own life. I was in a panic and called Dale, and after talking for some time he convinced me to contact the authorities.

I reluctantly called the police—I still wasn't sure that this was the right thing to do as I knew it would anger Philip and probably make things worse—and they sent an officer to check on him. The constable called me back and said he could not contact Philip and his car was not at the office. A few minutes later, he called again to say he'd found Philip's car tucked away in the back of the secure gated parking lot. I consumed a lot of good brandy as I waited for more news, but its quality was wasted on me. The constable kept pounding on the lobby door until Philip finally came down from his office on the second floor. Philip told the constable he was simply in a marriage breakdown and was not going to do anything to himself. Then he called me and said I had just made things worse by getting the police involved, and that he did not appreciate being interrogated by a twenty-four-year-old cop. At midnight, the constable called me one more time to let me know Philip was still there and had said he was going to get a hotel room for the night. Now all I could do was wait.

I think Philip's anger with and towards me was perhaps because he had finally realized that I didn't believe his lies anymore. Everything that went wrong in his life was always someone else's fault, and he would never admit he was wrong about anything. And for a long time, I had lived with my head in the sand and taken the blame. Now all I wanted was some truth in our relationship—I was still willing to work things out if he would just stop lying. As crazy as it was, I still loved him. I didn't want him to kill himself, but if he did, it would be his choice based on what he did, NOT what I did.

I spent the night in pure emotional agony, my heart pounding, unsure of what to do. The threats of suicide, the calls from the police, and the brandy kept me numb. I finally got to bed after the last call from the officer and managed to fall asleep.

Philip came home the following afternoon and I went to see if we could talk. Before I even opened my mouth, he said, "I don't want to talk to you. Stay away from me." For the rest of the evening, he stayed in one part of the house and I in another. He took himself to his camp in the spare bedroom for the night and left early the next day without saying a word. And as I sat in this empty, monstrous house—one I was only living in to make him happy—I wondered what I had done in my past life to have to deal with all this.

TEN

No Secrets

Between Philip's infidelity and my dad's passing, I was having trouble sleeping at night. In early November, Philip suggested that I go see my physician and ask for fifty Imovane to help me sleep. Truth be told, I think he wanted some of them for himself. He also suggested I say that the reason I needed them was because of all the travelling we did, likely in an attempt to keep our marital problems under wraps. But once I got to the appointment I thought, *What the heck*—one of my dear dad's favourite phrases—*I'm going to be honest.* My doctor had seen me through my previous marriage breakdown, so I knew he would be compassionate. And besides, I'm not a very good liar. People don't ask for sleeping pills for something trivial, and I would have hated to have him think I was trying to pull a fast one.

So, I told my doctor the real reason I needed those pills, and it turned out he was already aware of Philip's reputation. I didn't give him any names, but I gave him the general outline of the two women involved and all the lies that followed. I told him that Philip had suggested that we simply co-exist, and my doctor was very supportive and said I would have to think about whether or not that was something I could deal with. He also reminded me that I had been overly generous when I left my previous husband, and that I needed to make sure I would have a comfortable life without Philip if that was the road I took.

When I told him I only had my sister-in-law to talk to, my doctor told me I could come back to talk to him any time and recommended a society which he said had good counsellors. However, I didn't really want anyone else to become involved in this little soap opera I was living in. I even made my doctor promise complete secrecy, particularly because his wife was on the city council. As I left his office I thought, *I bet that little disclosure made his day!*

I did as my doctor suggested and put some thought into what my next steps might look like. For me, I needed to be the one and only in the life of the person I loved. I didn't care about having all the finest things in life; I just wanted to love and to be loved. For all his faults, I did still love Philip and think he was a great man in many ways—he had created all of SomaLife's products, after all. What I really wanted was for him and me to have a nice, long talk about how to move forward, but it was so difficult to have a meaningful discussion with him about any of this. He hated talking about what I needed from him and was always on the precipice of walking out of the room so he wouldn't have to deal with it.

Another thing that made it difficult for us to communicate was that Philip kept himself so busy. He always wanted more out of life, and he worked as much as he could so that he could have as much money coming in as possible—some of which was stashed in secret bank accounts for his personal use. I remember a postcard he was given by a close friend many years ago just to show how well she knew him. The postcard showed a man on a treadmill, and just out of his reach were women, cars, money, and all the things that indicate success. It was an apt representation of Philip's approach to life. All his hobbies, all his pursuits, cost money, and even with both our incomes it seemed we never had enough. The small income SomaLife was paying me went to the household expenses while Philip's income paid the mortgage, which we would never have had to take on if it weren't for all of his spending. The modest mortgage we had started out with had substantially increased to pay for another airplane and more cars. And when things went pear-shaped at SomaLife and we had to borrow money to keep the company afloat, it was always me who had to make the arrangements as I had the required credit rating and security.

In January 2008, we headed off for a six-day vacation in the Bahamas to see if we could reconnect. I had high hopes that this is what we needed to revitalize our relationship. It was our first real holiday in the twenty-three years we had been together—all our other travel had been whirlwind business trips or the occasional visit to see family in the UK. I was excited to get away to such a magical place and spend some time with just the two of us. The all-inclusive hotel was amazing, and our room looked out over the sandy beach and the ocean. The hotel had a big dining room with buffet tables overflowing with food yet still offered waiters to provide us with anything else we might ask for. The hotel also had individual dining rooms available: a Japanese restaurant, a steak house, and an Italian restaurant. We went for walks on the beach, swam with sharks, and searched for manta rays. We went snorkelling, had a photographer take some celebrity shots of us lying on the beach, and just enjoyed the tropical beauty of the landscape. That vacation was just what we needed, and I felt joy the whole time we were there. I had my wonderful husband back…for a week. When we got home it was back to business as usual and nothing much had been resolved. The frustrations continued.

I later found out that upon our arrival at the airport in Nassau, Philip had texted both Lena and Hanna. I will never understand how he could engage in this behaviour yet spend a very lovely time with me as if nothing else was going on.

We were now both at a point of being extremely frustrated with the situation and each other. Not long after our 2008 vacation, Philip wrote me an email:

Dear Marlies,

I guess that we have arrived at the inevitable impasse that two opposing viewpoints will always arrive at. I am tired of always being criticized by you about perceived deceptions. Here is an example: today I am off to present the latest medical guideline that we put together in record time on my last visit. This guideline will drive better quality medical care throughout the province and is an achievement that I am proud of. I am good at this sort of stuff, and I am tired of being criticized for doing these things. Things such as chairing the provincial Cancer Network, an organization devoted to engaging [family practitioners] more in the ongoing care of cancer patients and which produces practice management flow sheets to make that job easier, as well as a host of other things. Even being chosen to head up these types of organizations over the 4,000 other [general practitioners] in the province is quite an honour as those at the top of medical organisations and government recognise that I have the abilities and qualifications to do that. I always try to make the best use of the time away, so I combine, for example, a task with a meeting to maximise the visit even though this often means an evening meeting when I am tired and a later than usual night with the usual early rise to get to the airport early to catch the first flight back.

The same principles apply to the work I do in Alberta. I was always a good teacher at my medical school once I had qualified and was specialising, and I have always enjoyed pushing the quality of care forward to improve the lot of patients. My practice is another example. My patients receive top quality care of which I am also proud, but it takes a lot of work and going the extra mile. I am tired of being criticized there too. The other company, SomaLife, is another example; it could not, would not, exist without me and will fall if I disappear. For Weston, dealing with the suppliers when he does not know what he is doing is irksome. The non-signed off label is a good example. He seems to hold things close to his chest. I said on Tuesday at the meeting that I needed to talk to a formulator. I have not heard anything since. If we want to get a sports drink out ahead of the pack, time is of the essence.

Enough of me for the moment. I understand your situation and can sympathise and can only apologize for the grief I caused. For my part, it is easier to live in a little fantasy world of non-criticism than to be always under the gun. The old Jags and Rovers are a tiny part of what we have as assets and slowly restoring them brings some pleasure. Unfortunately, you do not share that enthusiasm but look on it all as liabilities. I have not flown for months, another thing I used to enjoy. There is no time between the practice, getting home, and travels. Finishing off the plane was not cheap, but at least there is now a nice little aircraft that I can enjoy one day perhaps. There are many things that we need to sort out, but I do not want you constantly chasing around looking for things that are not really there and drawing conclusions before I have had a chance to explain, although that does not seem to help either. I, like you, am defeated. We need to sort this out once and for all this weekend or tomorrow night when I am back from [Vancouver], a day on call, and the walk-in clinic.

This whole letter sounded like more of a resume than any effort to resolve our issues and differences. Philip was always quick to tell me how hard he worked and all the lives he was saving. He made it sound like he was so hard done by in order to guilt me into feeling bad about telling him what I needed. I wanted my Prince Charming back, but I wasn't sure how to make that happen. I responded:

Dear Philip,

I know that all your committees are important to you, and I believe you when you say you are making a difference. You are thought of highly by your patients for your competence and that is due to your exceptional caring for them. About always feeling criticized, I fully understand because I have felt the same way for years through being called stupid among many other things that were personally hurtful. You are wrong about me not having an interest in your restoration of cars. You never included me with these projects as YOU thought I would not be interested. At this point, the airplanes and cars, in my mind, are liabilities if it affects the overall picture of our financial security. Toys are expensive hobbies. For me, it always comes down to the financial picture as we always seem to be in overdraft, and I have a constant concern that the money will not be there for the big expenses that are always looming. All the money I earn goes into our joint account to help deal with bills. When I was on my own, I never had those insecurities.

We can talk about this on the weekend and whatever is decided upon, at least we had a wonderful time in Nassau last month. I will cherish that time as it was the first time in so many years that we had fun together and there was hope.

During our weekend chat, I asked him how I could trust

him to be true to me in the future. His answer was that he was "too tired and too old" to carry on with what he had been doing. I replied that four months earlier, he hadn't been too tired or too old to play two women at the same time. We left it at that and each went to our own bed. I still thought he should be the one who should be making a huge effort to make me feel loved and desirable. He was the one who messed up. Why didn't he get this? Maybe if he tried to understand, to hear what I was saying to him, we could move forward.

After this chat, I drove up to a ski condo we owned and rented out in the ski season, which I had listed for sale after learning about Lena—I did not want them to have a cozy little nest they could use as a getaway. I needed to clear it of all our personal belongings, and this trip would also give me time on my own to think. I started by cleaning out the garage and then moved through the condo. Most of what we had there was for the renters to use during their ski vacations, so I just spent a lot of time reminiscing and feeling sad that I was giving up what had been a fun ski getaway for a few years. We used to put the music video channel on the TV and hope for a cloudy day so we could stay inside, read, use our hot tub, and generally relax. Now, this place would just be a memory—another once joyous thing that disappeared from my life.

ELEVEN

Sharing the Secret

Being so unhappy and lonely was becoming too much to bear. As much as I didn't want to advertise my personal drama, I needed to share what was going on with someone I could trust. I decided to confide in a close friend from my dragon boat team, Emily, whom I had known since 2001. We started to go out for regular dinners at our favourite Japanese restaurant, and she was so wise and supportive. When I gave her a hint of what had been going on, she got tears in her eyes. She also read into my words that there was still hope on my part, and that I was trying to keep our marriage going despite his behaviour. She told me that there was a life out there for me, and that I had to ask myself why I was still in this marriage and whether I prepared to stay just to avoid being alone. In truth, I was already alone, but I wasn't ready to leave just yet.

Emily couldn't help me financially, but she said she would support me in any other way—even offering me a key to her condo if I felt Mom and I needed a place to stay. She also told me I had an aura that showed I was beautiful both inside and out, and I really needed to hear that. She always knew what to say to make me feel better.

Then, the day came when things went from bad to worse. Philip and I had an argument about all the CEOs he had hired to run SomaLife. These men had been using the company as their personal funding vehicle; we were basically paying for their lavish lifestyles. Most of them wanted me out of the company so that I couldn't reveal to the board what was going on, but I was the cofounder, for God's sake! At this time we were on CEO number five, and I told Philip he needed to get rid of this man before he ran the company into the ground. Philip was angry because I was questioning his judgement, and perhaps because he felt he could not get rid of him—he did not want to share my misgivings about how the company was being run with the board as it would reflect poorly on him. Suddenly, Philip lost control. He jumped up, left the room briefly, came back into the room pointing his .45 Magnum at me. He kept walking around the living room and shouting at me with his gun in his hand. I didn't know whether or not it was loaded and I didn't want to find out, so I just sat quietly and listened to him rant until he finally calmed down, left the house, and drove off.

As soon as he was gone, I ran out of the house with Rover, my German Shepard, and hid in the bushes in the empty lot next door for what seemed like a long time. I was terrified. Once I had calmed down, I went back inside; Philip returned home soon after. I didn't see the gun anymore, but I was still scared, and he was clearly shaken up by what he had done. He said he was sorry, but I was not so sure about his sincerity—while he had never done anything like this before, pulling that gun out had seemed too easy for him. I made him go get the gun and give it to me so I could hide it, although he later found it and hid it somewhere else. I never did report this incident to the police as I knew he would have been in real trouble and I wanted to protect him from himself. He was so shaken and apologetic that I didn't think he would do it again; that being said, I decided to stop pushing his buttons.

As I was trying to make sense of it all, Valerie revealed that she thought his lack of conscience was genetic on his father's side. Their father used to have an incredible temper, which cooled as he grew older, and he was sometimes physically violent with their mother when they were very young. Her mum, she said, was self-centred in her own way, but because she was very sweet and kind it almost went unnoticed. Knowing about these influences gave me some insight into a potential source of Philip's behaviour.

During my next dinner with Emily, she encouraged me to take things seriously and prepare for the worst. She reminded me that I was responsible for his lifestyle and that he wouldn't have our house or the same level of personal freedom if it wasn't for me. She was sure he already had an exit strategy, and she suggested I take the steps to protect myself financially. She even offered to take time off work to go see a lawyer with me. She also made me promise not to let him give me injections or pills of any kind. I told her about the sleeping pills that I had been on for the past four months, and she told me to quit right now—it sounded so foreboding, but she just wanted me to be careful. That was the last time I took a sleeping pill.

Having less and less faith in my future with Philip, I considered taking Emily's advice. Dale had recommended a good lawyer an hour out of town who apparently delighted in taking doctors to the cleaners. This wasn't exactly what I had in mind, but I knew Philip had access to the best lawyers due to his standing in the medical community so I would need a shark in my corner if we went that route. Emily had also suggested I hire a private investigator to find out who he might be meeting with outside of our marriage and thought the lawyer would be able to help me with that. However, I wasn't quite ready to pull the trigger just yet. Instead, I bought a GPS tracker and put it in the passenger side door pocket of his car so that I could see where he went. I was able to track him to Lena's place, and when I would call him to ask him where he was, he always lied. He eventually found the tracker while cleaning his car and I never saw it again, but now he knew that he'd been caught once again.

A month later, I decided to talk to Philip about all the thoughts swirling through my head and my inability to get beyond his betrayal. I told him that if the rest of our lives together was only going to bring more of the same insulting behaviour and lack of intimacy on his part, I did not want to do it. I asked him if he just wanted to be together because of the "stuff" we had accumulated, and he said he could live in a box with just his books. I didn't believe that for a minute. I then asked him what he really wanted, and he responded that he wanted peace in his life, the time to do the things he wanted to do, and to not have to work so hard. I didn't see myself in any of his wants.

I pointed out that he wasn't even trying to get me back on board after the mess he had created, and his response was that it takes two. In my mind, though, there were not two of us in this equation. He had made me feel like nothing, yet he wanted me to accept that his game-playing had not meant anything to him. He didn't give me many hugs, attempt to do anything together, or make an effort to heal the deep hurt that was still burning inside me. He simply maintained that his affairs had no substance. He could not say he loved me, but he did say that he would not still be here if it wasn't what he wanted. He said we should give the marriage a try, but as Yoda said, "Do or do not, there is no try."

I felt like I was stuck between a rock and a hard place. I did not want to continue in a loveless relationship, but I also did not want to leave. SomaLife and the people involved with the company were always on my mind; I could not bear for our distributors and shareholders to lose their income and investments if the company folded due to our personal situation. I also truly believed—and still do—in the incredible benefits of our Youth Formula, and I didn't want it to disappear from the world.

I wondered what my dad would have thought of this mess. He was such a man of character and integrity, and I wonder if he would have been disappointed in me. While my dad was no longer around to discover the truth of what was happening, my mom, who was so recently widowed, needed to be protected from the knowledge that I was so unhappy. She had occasionally commented on the fact that Philip was rarely home, and sometimes I thought she intuited more than she let on. She would be devastated to know her "little girl" was in so much emotional pain, and her feeling of safety in her final years was of the utmost importance to me. She shouldn't have to worry about me.

I could not let things continue the way they were—I had to get this thing turned around. It was time for me to stand my ground.

TWELVE

Living the Lie

At this point, Philip and I had settled into an impasse. He continued to come and go as he pleased and was secretive about everything he did, although I believed that most of it was rather mundane—just getting up to date on his work and perhaps spending some time on his cars and plane, which he couldn't afford and didn't have time to enjoy anyway. The good times were few and far between, by his choice.

As I continued to work on trying to move past Philip's infidelities, I still found myself asking questions in an attempt to understand why all of this had happened. Why did he feel the need to live in a fantasy? Why did he continue to deny what he had done when I had proof? Why didn't he just leave? Why, why, why?

In my search for answers, I had found and joined an online support group and was incredibly relieved to discover I wasn't alone—that there were many others who were struggling with the same issues. I posted about my situation, and I received an overwhelming amount of support. The people reminded me that this was not my fault, and that I had done nothing to provoke this. They said Philip had a God complex, and that his poor reaction to my accusations was due to him not wanting to lose control over his world. They told me that he likely wouldn't change, to go see a lawyer, and to take steps to protect myself, reaffirming the advice given to me by Emily.

It was time for the secrets to stop—all of them. I decided go see that out-of-town lawyer, the one who hated doctors, and get his advice on what responsibilities Philip had toward me. This was particularly important as I had guaranteed all his loans—at least the ones I was aware of—and if he went down, I would go down too. I wasn't necessarily planning to leave, but I had always believed that knowledge is power. I could only hope that if Philip understood that I had finally taken steps to protect myself, he might be forced to re-evaluate his priorities and become more forthright and honest in his dealings with me.

When I finally went to see the lawyer, I found him to be quite strange. He came across as being very offhanded about everything. He said what I was experiencing were just irritations—no big deal in the grand scheme of things. He also said if I went for a divorce there would likely be a fifty-fifty payout on the assets, which I would have thought fair in any case. The trouble was that Philip had gotten us into so much debt that we would have to sell everything to make it work—even the house that Philip seemed to be so attached to. On top of that, the lawyer calculated that Philip would have to pay me between $5000 and $7000 per month indefinitely as his part of the spousal support. I didn't think I could do this to him. I knew what our financial situation was, and by putting this burden on Philip, I would be hurting myself and everyone else I cared about—it was important for SomaLife that we remained on an even keel. The lawyer gave me the name of a counsellor, and when I told him Philip does not believe in counselling, he suggested I go on my own to get my perception straightened out. I had not realized that it was my perception that was the problem!

The visit with the lawyer had been unproductive. I paid him four hundred dollars for an hour and a half, and I was no better off than before. Regardless, I was determined to keep moving forward. The bottom line was that if there was to be any chance at all for our marriage, Philip needed to talk with me and be open to dealing with all this. He needed to be part of the solution—not only in resolving the betrayal created by his affairs, but also in getting our finances back in order. It was hard to get my head around what could be done to improve things when I was constantly worried about juggling all the accounts.

One night, before dinner, I told him that we needed to talk before we visited his son and daughter-in-law a few days later. He responded that if I didn't want to go, then I shouldn't; I told him his attitude did not solve anything. He finally agreed to talk, with the caveat that whatever happened to us would be up to me, although he wanted to "try" to make it work. His unenthusiastic response was not a good start.

I asked him if he thought trust and honesty were important in a marriage, and he said yes. I told him that all his business dealings outside of his medical practice—patients would occasionally approach him to invest in their businesses and he always lost money in the process—and all the "family" money he was spending made me uncomfortable, as well as the loans he was committing to without my knowledge. He was jeopardizing my financial security through all this spending, and he was the only one who benefited from it. I told him that whether I agreed or disagreed with what he was doing, I had a right to know what was being spent and when. He said he would keep me informed—his only contribution to the conversation thus far.

I also told him he had to set some boundaries around how

friendly he was with others. For example, a woman had recently come up to him at a party and kissed him on the lips—that couldn't happen anymore. He claimed that he couldn't help it, that she had come at him, but I didn't buy it. No one would ever kiss me on the lips if I didn't want them to. I also told him I sent an email to one of the women at the party and told her she had no respect for me or for him. He thought it was unfair of me to do that as her husband might see it, but at the time I didn't care what it would do to her marital relationship. After all, she was the one crossing the line.

Looking back now, I can admit that I shouldn't have done that. It was not what a mature person would do. It just seemed everyone else's feelings were more important than mine, and I let my hurt make decisions for me.

Finally, I asked Philip not to say things to me that he did not mean. When he asked for an example, I said, "Like saying you want me out of your life." He didn't respond to that one. The conversation ended at that point, with nothing being truly resolved. It was disheartening, to say the least.

I discussed this conversation with his sister after the fact, and she thought he just wanted things to carry on as normal with as few waves as possible—something Valerie said was a family trait. She pointed out that he had stuck things out when he could have easily left for one of the other women, which said it all. She said he wanted to stay with me, he just wasn't that demonstrative by nature, and he probably just needed time to unravel all his unnecessary complications with Lena and Hanna. The only way forward, she thought, was to put the past behind us and move on to the good life we both deserved. Valerie had always been a great source of support for me, but looking back now I can see that she was also very supportive of Philip, and that her words made me second-guess myself. After talking with her, I wondered if maybe she was right, and that I was expecting more than he could give. Maybe what he was offering me *was* his best. And things could have been worse, at least he never raised his hand to me.

At that point, I finally *truly* accepted that things may never get better with Philip. And as terrible as this decision sounds, it seemed to finally open up an opportunity for healing.

I ended up booking us a weekend trip to Penticton, about a forty-five-minute drive from our home, for our seventeenth wedding anniversary. I reserved a room with a Jacuzzi tub in the middle of it, and the hotel had a casino attached. I had wanted us to redo our marriage vows, but I was worried that this might get people thinking about why and I didn't want that drama for either of us.

We ended up having a wonderful trip. We had dinner at a restaurant overlooking the lake, then took a stroll before returning to the hotel. We went into the casino and played some of the slot machines. At the end of the night I had a couple of toonies left to gamble before we retired, so I put them both into the last machine as we were heading out the door. Suddenly, there were lights and sirens; I had just hit the jackpot of five thousand dollars! What a great way to end the evening. I took this as a good omen.

Even though things seemed to be settling down, I finally took the advice of both my doctor and the lawyer and went to see a therapist. At the end of the session, we both came to the conclusion that I had talked things through with Philip as much as I could, and now I just wanted this whole situation to be over with and for us to move forward. The only way I could be part of the solution was to be positive in my outlook and show that even though he been unfaithful, I still wanted to be with him. It does not do any good to say you will try to work things out if in fact you are so angry that it colours how you view everything. One must decide either to be there and forgive or to get out.

After months of turmoil, of frustration, of searching for answers, the red-hot anger I had been feeling was finally gone. I hoped the other two women were gone as well—I really didn't know one way or the other, but I had to believe they were or I would have a tough time moving forward. What I did believe was that if Philip did not want to be with me, he would be gone, and that was enough for me to get past the hurt and forgive. Yes, maybe some of it would be faking it 'til we made it, but it was worth a try if it meant our relationship could have a happy ending. I had to let the anger go and let healing begin instead of feeding the fire of betrayal and distrust. We had to arrive at a fair-value relationship together.

Healing can only begin when you can forgive—not just when the anger, bitterness, hurt, and pain are gone. I had finally come to see that I was standing in the way of my own healing, and that we are the only ones who can change our own minds and our hearts. I didn't want to live my life being angry all the time, and I was the only one who could let that anger go.

It had been a tough eight months, but I was finally seeing a glimmer of light at the end of the tunnel. It also helped that it was nearly spring, and soon all of nature would be renewed with the return of the swallows and the growth of our flowers and trees. The sun would radiate a new warmth, and life would go on.

And then, all that hope disappeared.

Things had been looking up. Philip and I were still communicating mostly by email, but he was a little more willing to talk and a little less stuck in denying what he had done. I was feeling better about our relationship now that

I had let go of all that anger, and I was starting to become hopeful again. However, my intuition told me that I had not seen the last of Lena. Now, I am ashamed to say this, but I hired a detective to check on him, and when he would fly off places I would drive out to the airport to see if the two of them arrived back together from wherever he had been. I was never surprised to see them together. On one such occasion, I parked next to his car as I waited. I saw him leave the terminal, and then a few seconds later I saw Lena exit as well. They never ever came out together, as if they would fool anyone who knew them with this charade. Philip got into his car without talking to me and began preparing to drive off, so I just drove back to his office as I knew he had patients coming in that afternoon. I waited for him in the gated parking area at his office, and when he arrived, all he could say was, "Well?" Unbelievable! I didn't want to cause a scene, so I drove off and left him there.

After that, I just gave up. I made no further efforts to improve our relationship, and I resigned myself to living separately in the same house so that I could remain a part of SomaLife. I could not bear to see it flounder and fail. Even with all that was happening, SomaLife and the success of our Youth Formula still brought me so much joy, so I decided to focus all of my efforts on making this company succeed.

THIRTEEN

Taking It to the Next Level

For the most part, the next seven years were fairly calm. I kept my focus on work and on doing things I enjoyed, such as dragon boating. In my fifties I had learned to steer a forty-five-foot-long dragon boat holding twenty paddlers, a drummer, and myself, and I still kept it up. I loved it, and I was good at it. My all-women's team went on to win countless medals, and our team became very well known throughout BC.

I also had plenty to keep me busy at the SomaLife office. At the beginning of this timeframe we had seventeen staff in place, so I could choose to do the things I liked to do. I would spend hours following up on declined credit cards and oversaw the customer service staff. We created a weekly update for our distributors to keep them informed about sales or any new happenings in the company—I would compile the contents of the update and even wrote a few articles myself, and then our graphic designer would make it look stunning and professional. I loved working with her as I could use some of my creativity. The company grew, but I sacrificed my social life in the process. I have since learned that you can't buy time, and I will never get back the time I lost with friends and family. I regret now that they became a missing piece of my life.

One of the other jobs I had taken on was arranging distributor events for the company. These provided people with an opportunity to meet the doctors and the staff, and they included informative health sessions, entertainment, and fun activities. Organizing these events entailed finding a suitable venue, finding guest speakers and entertainment, deciding on decorations, bringing in catering, and promoting the event to our distributors. I actually organized three successful events in Las Vegas, Seattle, and Kelowna, with the last one being the most memorable. I brought in some local Taiko drummers and learned to drum one song, so the event opened with the loud pounding of drums and with me playing front and center alongside this group of accomplished drummers.

That wasn't the only memorable part of the night. Towards the end, I was chatting with one of the guests when someone came running up to me—another guest had collapsed on the dance floor and was lying there unconscious and not breathing. I ran to get the doctors, who immediately sprang into action. One of them did mouth-to-mouth while Philip began chest compressions. The man did not respond. There was no defibrillator available in the hotel, so the doctors continued performing CPR for the eighteen minutes it took an ambulance to arrive while many of us formed a prayer circle around the scene. By the time the guest was wheeled away, the doctors were completely exhausted. We later learned that the man had experienced a heart attack and was put on an air ambulance to Victoria, BC, to have open heart surgery. Thankfully, he not only survived but went on to make a full recovery.

It was times like these when I saw what a talented doctor Philip was, and I was so proud of him. It was also times like these that made me question if I was asking too much of him—if I should just accept him exactly as he was.

Not everything was easy over those years, though. As mentioned before, our CEO at the time—the Englishman who had seemed so promising at the start—was slowly running us into the ground. Our staff of seventeen dwindled down to just five people, myself included. Then the CEO moved to the States, which made him completely incapable of running the company, and in 2012 we let him go.

Once the news got out, Glenn—the marketing guru who had disappeared after the CEO had stopped paying him—returned and made overtures about becoming part of the company again. After seeing his marketing plans, Philip welcomed him back into the company to work with the COO on moving the company forward.

Glenn would show up every so often and have meetings with Philip in which he was supposed to bring us up to date on what had been achieved. However, Glenn didn't give much information on what he had being doing to increase business and whether or not it had been successful, instead making huge promises about what he could do if we put him in charge. He told Philip that if he had control, he would set up nine or ten other related companies that would create revenue under the umbrella of SomaLife. He claimed that this would bring in more investors and help the company grow once again. For this to work, our existing SomaLife shareholders would have to switch their shares to his American company, including all the shares Philip and I had held as the major shareholders. Glenn was a real talker—some may say a flimflam man—and convinced Philip that this would be a wise choice. With this move, Philip, having the majority of the shares, gave the company—MY company—away. I didn't have a lot to say about this whole transaction, but if Glenn could make the company grow again, then I was happy.

Before the transfer went through, I asked Glenn if I could stay on as president of the company. I held this role in name only—I had not been required to do anything presidential in quite some time, and I was still being kept in the dark about important financial decisions. Thankfully, Glenn agreed; it was a relief to still be involved in the company. However, as Glenn now had the majority of shares in his name, I did not feel I had the power to make any changes, and that suited his needs just fine.

There was barely time to process this shift before our lives changed in the worst possible way. Over the previous eight years, Philip had often complained about a hernia he had and the pain it was causing him, yet he didn't want to take the time to get it surgically repaired. Finally, the pain became so bad that he decided to have it dealt with. This was just a day surgery and he should have had an easy recovery, requiring only a few days off work, but it was weeks before he felt well enough to return to his office. After about a week of going to the office every day, I received an ominous phone call from him. He said he was in so much pain that he could feel every bump in the road as he was driving to work, so he had gone to the hospital to have it checked out.

After a few days and a variety of tests, he was given a diagnosis: pancreatic cancer. This was devastating news. I had heard of so many other people who had died from this disease—including Patrick Swayze, one of my favourite actors—but I had never heard of anyone surviving it.

Shortly after he received the diagnosis, we sat on our balcony one evening and watched the stars flicker on one by one. We were very quiet for a while, each of us lost within our own thoughts. Eventually, I quietly asked if this was the end, and he agreed that yes, it was. I told him I could only see him through this if I knew that Lena was no longer in the picture; he assured me that she hadn't been in the picture for a long time. I wasn't sure if I believed him, but I did know that he was going to need a lot of care. For better or worse, I had to look after him.

Having been the chief of staff at Kelowna General Hospital for the past eighteen years, Philip was given the royal treatment. He was allowed to finish up some things at his office, and a few days later he was scheduled to have a surgery called a Whipple procedure. They would go in and remove part of his pancreas, a portion of his small intestine, his gall bladder, and his bile duct in an effort to stop the spread of the cancer and perhaps save his life.

Finally, the day of the surgery arrived. I walked next to his gurney as far as I could and wished him well as the orderly rushed him into the operating room. I didn't know how long the procedure would take, so I went home alone and waited for his surgeon to call and update me. At midnight, four hours after the surgery started, I finally got the call that he was in recovery. I returned to the hospital to find him almost sitting up in bed in the Intensive Care Unit with a big smile on his face. He showed me the incision—a huge inverted "V" across his stomach. He was in such good spirits that I thought that maybe, just maybe, the doctors had fixed him. After all, he was being looked after by the best there was, and I was sure he was not ready to leave us.

Unfortunately, things don't always go the way we want them to. While the surgeons had done the best they could, the cancer had already spread. He was given nine months to live. As Philip's health continued to decline, he opted to have chemotherapy—even though we both acknowledged that there was no cure for pancreatic cancer, I think he was hoping that that he could extend his life a bit. I would drive him to the hospital for the treatments and pick him up hours later, then watch him suffer from the nausea and general illness. When he came home between hospital visits, often all he could do was to sit in his comfy chair and sleep. Home care nurses came in daily to take care of his ports and dressings, and I made him a bed on the couch as he didn't have the energy to move downstairs to the room he had taken over years ago. I could see the life draining out of him as he shrank into a smaller version of himself daily. The bones in his back began to show, and he started losing what little hair he had left. He was always cold, so I bought him a full-length down coat so he might still be able to sit out on the patio for a few minutes and get some fresh air. Finally, the oncologist declined to give him further treatment as he was too weak to withstand it.

After the fact, some of Philip's friends commented that they had noticed his jaundiced skin over the summer and thought he was not at all well. However, none of them brought it up with him, and as someone who saw him every day I had not noticed the slow change. To this day, I wonder if someone speaking up would have made a difference in his prognosis.

Philip was diagnosed at the beginning of October, and by the middle of December he spent all his time in bed. I eventually set him up by a bay window in the living room so he could at least have a pleasant view of the lake. As his body continued to weaken, his cognitive function began to decline as well.

The beginning of the end came soon after. I heard movement around midnight one night and went to check on Philip. He had managed to get out of bed and was trying to walk with his walker, perhaps to go to the bathroom. When I tried to help him, though, he was incoherent and did not respond. He sat on his chair, but then he did not have the strength to get back up and return to his bed, and I was unable to lift him despite his significant weight loss. I didn't know what to do. I knew he did not want me to call an ambulance, but I felt I had no choice. I just wanted them to help me move him back into bed. When they saw what I was trying to deal with, though, they made the decision to take him back to the hospital.

When I went to visit him the next day, he was a little more alert—he had been dehydrated, and some intravenous fluids had remedied that. That morning, his doctor called me into the hall and told me that Philip only had days left. It was recommended that he be moved into hospice; I don't know why, but Philip had always said this was something he never wanted to do. I begged his doctor to allow him to stay in the hospital that he had always been such a large part of, especially as he had been given a private room. Thankfully, they agreed.

That afternoon, he was moved upstairs to another private room and the vigil began. I contacted his youngest son, who was now a captain for Cathay Pacific, and told him that he needed to come home immediately to say his goodbyes. He arrived from Hong Kong December 15 with his wife and two children. Philip's eldest son, who lived in Kelowna, was also there with his wife and son. We were a sombre little group waiting for the inevitable. I spent all my time at the hospital now, and the nurses kindly brought in a gurney for me to sleep on. I had to turn his patients away as he would not have liked them seeing him at the end. Only his closest friends, his squash partner, and our next-door neighbour were allowed in.

At the end of 2015, just seventy-six days after his diagnosis, my husband of thirty-one years passed away. Although I was deeply saddened, I also felt an immense sense of relief as I walked out of the hospital one last time. I had loved Philip despite everything we went through, but all I had wanted for so long was peace. Now I would finally get to experience that.

I would miss him, but I was also curious to see what my future would hold.

Philip's youngest son needed to return to Hong Kong, so I postponed the funeral and opted to wait and do a celebration of life. Three months later, we held the most beautiful celebration attended by many of his patients, colleagues, and local celebrities. The building was full, and through many tears, as well as some laughter, we all said our goodbyes.

In 2016, almost a year after Philip's death, I flew to England to attend the fifty-fifth reunion of the rugby team he had played on at the Portsmouth Grammar School. I stayed with Valerie, and the two of us hosted the rugby team's social event with a "tea" in her palatial home. I was well received and made welcome again by the team, whom I had met during a previous reunion five years prior. It was on that visit that I brought Philip back home to England. I had his ashes placed in a regular-sized urn as well as a matching mini urn, and I gave the smaller one to Valerie to see if it could be placed in the same grave that held this mother, father, and brother.

He was returning home.

FOURTEEN

Cleaning up the Mess He Left

Philip's death brought to light many issues that were left to me to clean up. For one, I soon found out I was the owner of seventeen cars in addition to the one I was driving, as well as having one-fifth ownership in an airplane. I spent a whole day with the Insurance Corporation of BC transferring every car into my name so I could dispose of them. I had no idea Philip had bought and hidden away so many cars—all needing work that he would never find the time to do—but that certainly explained all the money he was spending. I sold his share in the plane and the cars that were worth selling; I had several of the cars junked as they were too far gone to fix without spending thousands more. There is still a cute little MGB out there somewhere that I haven't been able to find; maybe someday someone will try to insure it and it will come back to me.

I also had to find and pay off all of Philip's personal loans, of which there were many. I had found it odd over the years that whenever SomaLife needed money, he would approach people he knew for loans rather than going to the bank and getting proper financing. It was also strange that the company always seemed to need money even though sales were good. I found out later it was because expenses incurred by management exceeded the deposits, yet no one seemed to be keeping track of this even though we had an accountant managing the money.

This prevented the company from borrowing as its own entity, so Philip or I would have to bail it out with personal funds.

There was one particular loan that I was less than thrilled to have to deal with: the loan from Lena out of her inheritance. Philip made her a sweetheart of a deal by adding ten percent to the loan amount, which was then supposed to be paid back over a five-year period. In addition, she was given shares in the company, which to me was insult on top of injury. I soon discovered that on top of the ten percent that had been added to her loan, the accountant was reducing her loan calculating repayment as principal plus interest. This meant that we were paying her interest twice, and that the loan was reducing a lot slower than it should have been. This was completely incompetent accounting on the company's end. After many payments had been made, SomaLife again experienced cash flow challenges and the payments to Lena ceased. Her financial advisor contacted Philip and accused him of perpetrating a scam, but Philip was able to deal with him somehow.

To appease Lena for having given him such a huge chunk of her inheritance, he signed over an airplane to her—a plane that they had been building together with their friends, with her acting as his money source and manager. I also found out that she had bought one of his Jaguars a month before he died; I wasn't sure if that was a legitimate sale or if it was part of him paying her off.

Philip had woven such a tangled web that I asked to have a meeting with Lena to sort everything out. I told her I would repay the balance of her loan at a nominal amount each month, and I kept to my word. However, it was incredibly difficult to keep our dealings civil. I had never been convinced that Lena was truly out of the picture, especially as there had been many indications that she was still working for him. I eventually found out that they had opened another office bank account that she had full access to, and that right after Philip died, she had cleared it out and closed it. However, none of this mattered anymore—there was nothing I could do now to change what had happened in the past—and I did what I needed to do to get her out of my life once and for all.

In the years following Philip's death, I kept busy by doing various renovations on the large home I was now rattling around in on my own. While this had always been Philip's house, I had grown to love living on the lake and didn't want another big upheaval in my life, so I chose to stay. And as I worked through the renovations, I began to make this place my own.

One of the biggest projects was completely gutting the two-car garage. Philip had put in a car lift so that he could work on his vehicles, which of course never happened. Now it was just in the way and took up a lot of space, so I had it removed and sold it. But that was just the beginning. There were numerous items hanging from every possible surface; I removed them all. The walls and ceiling were mudded and taped, then painted white. I had beautiful cupboards installed and put in an epoxy floor. At the end of it all, that garage was beautiful. I also got a stunning new front door with an oriental design and put in a huge walk-in closet in the master bedroom. I ripped out carpets and had laminate flooring put in. Finally, I changed the popcorn ceilings throughout the house to stretch ceilings from Germany, which made the rooms look twice as tall and reflected everything in the room below it. I described them as being like saran wrap on steroids. I found that I loved working with the trades, and it was therapeutic to renovate and beautify what I already had.

Sadly, life outside of the house was much more complicated. Glenn was still in charge of SomaLife, and his involvement appeared to be a massive waste of time. He would show up at the office at about two o'clock each day and claim that he had been "deep diving" into building business funnels and creating other marketing pieces until the early morning, none of which ever materialized. He would also have many meetings with potential business partners who later complained to me that their discussions never went anywhere.

Glenn did work with an investment fund manager to develop a program where people or businesses in Canada could invest retirement savings in SomaLife and get a rebate from the Canadian government. Unfortunately, I found out much later that the program was not set up properly and had been put on hold, putting the investments of these new shareholders in limbo. Obviously, the investors were not happy. Glenn was reluctant to let me know, particularly as I had invested a high six figures into this plan and was now about to lose it as well, but he couldn't hide it from me forever. The solution, as I was told by the fund manager, was for me to repay all the investors out of my pocket. He had created the problem, yet he expected me to fix it. I thought it was time to seek legal representation, and my legal team helped guide me through the process of saving SomaLife.

Unfortunately, this wasn't the only problem. As I would later find out, Glenn was funnelling funds out of the account to his wife in the USA to support her and his stepchildren. In order to have more money available to him, he began firing staff—soon, we were down to just him, me, and one customer service representative. Then, he started to ask me for personal loans, which made me feel uncomfortable. Asking me for a "loan" to pay off his mortgage in the USA was the last straw. It was time to go see a lawyer...again.

After meeting with the company's lawyer, I finally found

my voice and confronted Glenn. He turned out to be a coward and simply didn't return to work.

With Philip gone, it was now solely up to me to determine the future of SomaLife. And the more I thought about it, the more I realised that I was the best person for the job. I had never felt comfortable with any of the outside leadership Philip had brought in, and each person had put their own personal gain over the needs of the company. In contrast, I had always put the company first because I wanted nothing more than for it to succeed. And as I looked back, I could see that the times that SomaLife did best were the times when I was most involved in the company. I had spent so much time doubting myself thanks to the years of gaslighting; now, it was finally dawning on me that I had the power to lead the company all along.

In early 2019, I made the decision to call all my loans and, with legal help, put the company into receivership so I could get it back under my control. The company would not survive under Glenn's leadership, especially now that he didn't come in at all, and my company—my baby—would have been lost not just to me, but to all the people who had come to depend on our products over the years. I have always felt guilty that so many people may have lost their investment due to this decision, but as it was later pointed out to me, the company would have eventually folded anyway and everyone would have been in the same position. It was a difficult decision for me to make, but I knew it was the only way to move forward.

Before the receivership came into effect, I went to anyone who was owed money by the company and made a settlement offer. Lena was one of those people. I told her I was making arrangements to close the SomaLife office, and that I wanted to settle with the creditors prior to that so everyone at least got something. After consulting with her financial manager, she accepted my offer, and I had the satisfaction of being done with that uncomfortable chapter of my life.

Interestingly, though, Lena sent me a follow-up email shortly after where she tried to justify being with Philip all those years. She told me she had been afraid to leave him as she did not know what he might do; it was then that I realized that she had been a victim of his abuse as well. As with many of the other women in his life, he had used his charm to weave her into his web of lies. It was obvious she wanted to please him, even at the expense of her own family, and I am sure she was frustrated that her relationship with him never blossomed into something more. And while I managed to come out of this and rebuild my self-esteem by aligning myself with my family once again, Lena needed counselling together with a huge amount of support to build herself back up again.

I didn't like the person she was, yet I wished her a good life. We had both been pawns in a very nasty game, and now we needed to let go of all the blame we had placed upon ourselves and just get on to living a happy and honest life. I forgave her, and I was ready to move on.

FIFTEEN

An Ultimate Sense of Power

Most little girls dream of a fairy-tale romance followed by a fairy-tale wedding. But as I approached the end of my sixties, I'd had two weddings and no happily ever after. Both of my husbands had been challenging to live with, even abusive at times. One marriage had ended in divorce, the other remained rocky right until the end. I had resigned myself to making the best of what I had; I never would have guessed that this dream was finally about to come true for me.

In 2016, my sixty-ninth birthday was approaching. It looked like it was going to be just another lonely day as my family and friends were not available to help me celebrate, so I decided I needed to do something just for me. Soon, I felt an idea forming. I had previously owned a large automatic scooter—a Honda 650 Silver Wing—and I had a closet full of the cutest leathers for safe riding. Why not make myself feel better by going motorcycle shopping? It would be the ultimate retail therapy! I headed off to our local Harley dealer, and before I knew it I was the proud owner of a Harley Davidson Sportster. I didn't know how to change gears, having always ridden an automatic, so I had the motorcycle delivered to my house and left it to the universe to help me sort out that small challenge. I have always felt that when you truly believe in something, good things happen.

I continued to visit the Harley dealership on a regular basis to shop for T-shirts and other goodies to get ready for the day I would finally ride. During one such visit, one of the salesmen said he wanted to introduce me to someone. I followed him out to the parking lot where I could see motorcycle lessons in progress and was introduced to one of the instructors, who I was told could help me get on my bike and figure out the gears. Little did I know that this would be a new beginning in more ways than one.

This instructor, Bob, was not so much a knight in shining armor but rather a former cowboy. He provided me with one of the bikes he used in his classes that was similar in size to the one I had purchased. The first thing he taught me was how to use the clutch—I had driven a standard car in my youth, so I caught on very quickly. With that, my motorcycle riding began. Bob thought I would only need two hours of instruction before I could head off on my own, and that is what I paid for, but I found that first hour was really tiring. I had to balance, keep my feet off the ground, learn to use the clutch smoothly, and ride very slowly around cones on the parking lot. There was a lot to concentrate on. I asked him if I could take a raincheck on the second hour, and he agreed so long as he could come to my home to finish the lesson. That worked out quite well as I live on a quiet road that ends with a cul-de-sac leading to a resort, making it a good spot for a lesson.

The next day, under Bob's direction, I rode the bike back and forth over a couple of miles; I held up traffic a few times, but no one got too upset. At the end of the lesson, I thought that I could now practice on my own until I felt confident enough to go out in real traffic, so I thanked Bob and sent him on his way. I figured that would be the last time I saw my cowboy motorcycle instructor. I was wrong.

Apparently, I had made an impression. Bob confided in friends that he was interested in asking me out, but that he wasn't sure whether this would be appropriate or not as I had been his student. His friends assured him that a two-hour lesson hardly qualified as putting him in a position of power over me, so he gathered up his courage and asked me out.

For one of our first dates, we planned to take part in the Annual Vintage Bike Canyon Run out of Chilliwack. Bob's son, Stewart, was also an avid motorcyclist with a garage full of exotic cars and vintage motorcycles, and he decided to join us along with the love of his life, Shera-Lynn. They were newly dating, just as we were, so in essence it was a father/son double-date. We all drove down to Chilliwack, BC, in Stewart's truck, towing a trailer that held several of his vintage motorcycles. When we arrived, we met about forty to fifty riders in an open farm field who were all ready to take part in this adventure. The plan was to make our way to Hope for the first fuel stop, then head on to Lytton, and finally to Lillooet where the ride was to end with a big party at the town's Legion. There would also be an awards ceremony for the best vintage bike, which Stewart won every year. I wasn't ready to take a ride of this distance through winding and unfamiliar roads, so I kept Shera-Lynn company in the truck as we followed the riders.

It was a smoking-hot day, so when we arrived in Lytton we all gathered at a gas station to find some shade while we took a break. After a short stop, the riders once again got on the road while we followed along in the truck. This was not an easy road to drive on—it was only a single lane in either direction with lots of bumps and potholes—but the scenery was well worth it. The road was off the beaten path, nowhere near any busy highways, and the twists and turns made the ride even more interesting.

About twenty minutes into the ride, we lost sight of Bob and his son—Stew was a bit of a rebel with a need for speed, and the bikes could take the corners much faster than the truck. We were happily cruising along in the air-conditioned truck when about halfway between Lytton and Lillooet, we came upon a shocking sight. At first I did not register what I was seeing, but soon I processed the vision of a rider and his motorcycle lying in the northbound lane. Then I heard Shera-Lynn shout at me as she slammed on the brakes, "That's Bob!"

I quickly jumped out of the truck and ran to his side. As I saw the copious amounts of blood running down his face and into his helmet, I knew this was bad. I didn't want to move him, so I just gently lifted his visor so he could get air. Stew—who had just returned after noticing his father wasn't following him—took over and got his helmet off, which I wasn't happy about as we had no idea what the extent of his injuries were. Bob wasn't moving but seemed to be semi-conscious, trying to blink the blood out of his eyes. When he came to, he kept mumbling incoherently.

Some of the other riders had caught up with us now, and among them was a nurse who quickly assessed the situation. She tested to see if he could move his feet; thankfully, he could. We then had to decide our next course of action. Could we get cell phone service on this remote stretch of the road to call for an ambulance? If we did, could Bob wait for the hour or more that it would take for the ambulance to reach us and then drive him to the hospital? We did not know what his injuries were, only that there was a lot of blood. We finally decided it would be quicker if we transported him in the truck ourselves, even with the risks attached. We struggled to get him into the front seat of the truck, then I sat behind him to stabilize his position.

That drive was the longest twenty minutes of my life. His

brain seemed scrambled, and he kept asking the same three questions: "What happened? Is everyone alright? Did anyone get hurt?" I believe he thought I might have been on his bike with him as I had planned to join him at some point on the ride. I kept assuring him over and over that he had not harmed anyone other than himself.

When we finally arrived in Lillooet, two nurses helped us get Bob into a wheelchair and then quickly delivered him into an examination room. Once the temporary bandages we had used were taken off, we could see a deep cut across his nose and right cheek, almost slicing his face in half. Bob was still not very responsive, so he was taken for an x-ray and further assessment.

After the examinations were complete, the doctor determined that Bob might have a fracture of his spine and a concussion, and he knew for certain that Bob would need plastic surgery to deal with his facial wounds. However, they didn't have a doctor who could perform the required surgery— this was a very small town with a population of approximately two thousand people. Consequently, an ambulance was called to transport Bob to the Kamloops Regional Hospital one hundred and seventy kilometres away. I asked to go with him in the ambulance so that I could stay by his side. It was a slow ride, with more twists and turns, and Bob was in and out of consciousness as he had been given some heavy pain medication. Even though our relationship was in its earliest stages, I was glad that I was able to ride to Kamloops with him. I held his hand for the entire trip, and I don't know who needed that more.

After a successful surgery, Bob remained in the hospital for three days, mainly for observation, while I stayed at a nearby motel. The doctors there had confirmed that he had a concussion and a compression fracture in his spine, and they put him on pain medication for it which he was not happy about. Every day, I would go to the hospital to be with him and help him with anything he wanted or needed. When I was tired, I would get up on the bed with him just to be close to him and get some rest.

At first the accident made absolutely no sense as Bob, with his lifetime of experience, was really the best and safest rider in the valley. Eventually it was determined that Bob had suffered from heat stroke on that hot ride, likely due to being dehydrated, which had caused him to pass out. This was probably a good thing as he would have been in a relaxed state when he hit the pavement face-first, much like a ragdoll, potentially saving him from even more broken bones. He managed to give everyone a scare, but because he was a responsible rider and dressed for a slide, he made it through just fine.

Once Bob was discharged, I needed to get back home as I had been away from the office since before the weekend. Bob's youngest son, Darren, drove to Kamloops from Kelowna and picked both of us up to bring us back home. Bob was living on his own at this time, and given the recovery process for his injuries and the time it would take him to heal, I thought it would be best if he stayed with me. That way, I would be there to look after him until he felt well enough to be on his own again.

Over the course of the next three years, Bob and I went on many adventures and explored the countryside on our motorcycles. We also joined the Annual Vintage Bike Run the next two years, although this time I was doing the riding as well. The more time we spent together, the deeper our relationship became. Bob was the kindest man, he respected me, and he made me feel like I was the most important person in his life. It was so rewarding to meet a person who measured their words, spoke with kindness, and loved sharing their knowledge.

In 2019, the party at the end of the Vintage Bike Run was once again held at the Legion in Lillooet, and after a few beers and tequila shots we decided that it might be nice to get married. He spent so much time at my place anyway, and we enjoyed each other's company. It was an easy decision to make.

On September 29, 2019, we had our fairy-tale wedding at a western cabaret. I wore cream-coloured cowboy boots covered in rhinestones and a matching Stetson with a shoulder-length veil flowing down the back, held on to the brim's band by three stars in a circular rhinestone-encrusted broach. My sleeveless dress was also cream coloured and knee length, and I wore a long lace duster to finish off the elegant western look I had been striving for. I felt beautiful. We kept the ceremony itself simple, with just our best man, Don, and his wife, Susie, who I jokingly referred to as my flower girl. I was walked down the aisle by my brother, and we had the most entertaining marriage commissioner we could have asked for. The cabaret was owned by one of our friends, who gave us the use of the entire venue to celebrate our special event. Friends and family came from far and wide, and everyone remarked that we probably had the wedding of the year. I felt like a princess, and there was finally peace in my kingdom.

SIXTEEN

Back on Track

After all the years of drama, I had finally found happiness and was working hard on getting the business back on track. Once I stopped the company from hemorrhaging money, I settled in and worked on streamlining our processes and payables. I was finally able to look into proper marketing and hired a company who could do all the things I needed help with and who actually delivered what they promised. I ordered the creation of a new website that is both user friendly and reflects my goals of a fair-value enterprise. Due to the improving health of the company, I was able to make a large donation for the Blind Children's Fund in Canada and rode my motorcycle in a week-long charity rally benefiting the Military Police Fund for Blind Children. I have donated another sizeable amount to West K Women of Influence, where I am a member, to help make up a Christmas hamper for a family in need. Money management is my superpower, and I am very proud of what I have achieved in just one year of being "under new ownership."

Shipping our products has always been a work in progress. We had been shipping supplements to our Canadian customers from our location in Canada and to our American customers from a fulfillment house in Atlanta, Georgia. In 2019, we got a notification from our American fulfillment centre that our shipping volume wasn't high enough, giving us a month to find another distribution provider. We made a lot of frustrating phone calls and performed many fruitless online searches in an attempt to find a fulfillment house that was affordable and offered the services we needed, and it soon became clear that the transition to a new facility was going to cost a lot of money. So, I made the decision to have all the inventory at our American fulfillment centre shipped up to Canada. Doing this saved the company a lot of initial setup money as well as the ongoing fees and expenses the centres charge, and it also allowed me to manage all our inventory from one location, putting everything totally in my control.

Things were finally, FINALLY, looking up. Then, of course, 2020 hit.

The first hint I had of a possible pandemic came just before I took a vacation to Mexico in late January. I was running SomaLife with just one customer service representative, Kim, who has been with the company since 2014. I don't know what I would do without her. She does more than just customer service; she is a problem solver who fills all the orders, looks for ways to market our products, writes marketing drafts, and is loved by our customers because of the extra care she takes with each and every one of them. I knew she would take great care of the company while I was gone. There had been some news about the city of Wuhan and something called a coronavirus, but I didn't pay any attention to it until I arrived at the airport in Puerto Vallarta to find several of the immigration officers wearing face masks. I wasn't overly concerned about this, though, and I went on to have a fabulous vacation.

My first day back at the office was on February 20, 2020. At this point, everything still seemed relatively normal. Kim and I spent some time catching up—we had been communicating about work while I was gone but had not covered anything on a personal level—and then she told me she had a tumor or growth that would require extensive surgery. In the same breath, she also told me she had things all figured out so that we would lose very little time processing orders. As all our orders were online, Kim said she could do shipping from home if we could get her set up to do so.

As we waited for Kim to be given a surgery date, I had a brainstorm. I suggested to her that perhaps we should both work out of our homes rather than paying for an office for just the two of us. We had a fabulous bookkeeper, Brenda, who already worked from home, which told me that it was possible. Kim was planning on working from home after her surgery anyway, so why not make it permanent? I didn't realize it at the time, but I was putting all the pieces in place that would allow me to function in my own bubble.

Unfortunately, there was another wrinkle in the mix. For the past twenty years, Kim had been living in subsidized housing. When she first moved in, she had been a single mother with disabilities working for minimum wage with her young son in her care. Now, she had worked her way up to a position where she no longer needed or qualified for the subsidized housing. She was given a year to find a new place to live, so she set out to find and buy her first home. This was an exciting step for her, and I'd like to think I helped make this possible.

In March, Kim finally found a condo that she could afford. I was asked by the mortgage company to write a job confirmation letter, and in it I announced that she was making two dollars per hour more than her existing pay. Kim, of course, was ecstatic when she saw this.

I made the decision to give Kim a raise even knowing of the uncertainty we might soon be facing; she so deserved it, and I have absolutely no regrets. I had also made a deal with her a few months earlier that I would pay her for seventy-five hours every two weeks regardless of how many hours she actually worked. The only stipulation was that she "get the work done," and she has done that in spades! Looking after your staff pays the highest dividends, and Kim has always gone above and beyond for both me and the company. Her loyalty is a force to be reckoned with, and I cannot adequately express my gratitude for having her in my life. I am proud to have been able to more than double her wages in less than six years.

With all of this in place, Kim and I began exploring the possibility of working exclusively from home. I started making the calls to relocate our computers and printers to where they would be needed—the company that manages our data, firewalls, and general computer maintenance was instrumental in making the move seamless so that the business had absolutely no downtime. I had to close accounts, cancel my office lease, and physically move everything to our homes. In Kim's case, we had to do the move twice because the closing date on her new condo did not quite match up with what we were trying to accomplish. We thought of both moving out of the office at the same time, but staggering the dates meant the office did not have to be officially closed for the time it took to achieve the physical move and get everything back up and running. This cost a little more than doing it all at once, both timewise and financially, but in the long term it was worth it. We are now running very lean, and this entire adventure has given both Kim and me so much more free time—and as I said earlier, you can't buy time.

The move was completed near the end of March, just before all non-essential services were required to close. Because of the decisions I had made to bring everything in-house, we were able to keep functioning and get orders sent out seamlessly. I can only say that I believe I have a host of angels who directed me at the exact times I needed guidance to make the right decisions before disaster befell us.

In April, Kim was finally given notice that her surgery would take place a week later. She immediately went to work filling the recurring orders a little earlier than their due date so no one would be without their supplements during the short span of down time. This meant all her work was completed before she went in for her surgery. Kim was in the hospital for just three and a half days—the hospital did not want to keep anyone in longer than was necessary due to concerns around the coronavirus. I was surprised at the brevity of her hospital stay, but having her workspace at home helped give Kim plenty of recovery time with no pressure to get back to an office.

This certainly has been a challenging time—one we are still working through as I write this book—but I truly believe Kim and I are acing it. With the current pandemic, our strength lies in the fact that our loyal customers now have even more reason to continue using our supplements. Our flagship product has many health benefits including deeper restorative sleep, improved skin tone with a reduction in wrinkles, improved hair luster and strength, reduction of body fat (especially with exercise), better mood, and stronger and faster nail growth. But what is most important in this moment is that this supplement has the potential to strengthen your immune system—your first line of defense! As such, I started looking for ways to make sure it was affordable for our existing customers as well as new ones.

Our products are very expensive to manufacture as they are made with pharmaceutical-grade ingredients, so I knew that reducing that cost was a good place to start. For some time, our products had been manufactured in the US, then were shipped to Canada, and then sent back down to our American customers. After I moved all our inventory back up into Canada, I did some research and found a Canadian company in my neck of the woods who would manufacture some of our supplements based on Canadian prices. I then took a leap of faith that I would not fall flat on my face and made a larger-than-usual order so that I would be able to negotiate a better price. Today, our inventory is being produced at the lowest cost ever! I may be tooting my own horn, but I believe I was able to negotiate such a good price because I have created great relationships with my suppliers.

I am now able to trickle these savings down the line so that they benefit those who need it most. I have sent out emails to my customers providing a permanent across-the-board reduction in product pricing to help them continue their supplementation. I've also set up an affiliate program through which our customers can refer others and earn fifteen percent of those sales while their customers also receive fifteen percent off their orders. It's a win/win scenario!

After I made the decision to take over the company without all the previous management baggage, I started to look for ways to be able to showcase SomaLife as being new and improved. I have a vision of a vibrant company with a look that reflects my values, and I know I can't do it all on my own as I had when the company first started out. So, I asked for help. I now have people from *Shark Tank* of television fame in my corner, and I am happy to pay for their expertise. No more wasting resources, no more throwing mud against the wall to see what sticks. I feel confident that I can fulfill the legacy of good health for those discerning people who have grown to love our products and remain loyal customers and friends, and I am excited about SomaLife's future!

Even though these last couple of months have been filled with uncertainty, I feel blessed to be in the position I find myself in today. I can help others and still live my life the way I wish to live it and have come to love it, and that is a true blessing.

SEVENTEEN

Let It Go!

There was a man who had four sons. He wanted his sons to learn not to judge things too quickly, so he sent each of them in turn on a quest to go and look at a pear tree that was a great distance away. The first son went in the winter, the second in the spring, the third in summer, and the youngest in the fall. When they had all gone and come back, he called them together to describe what they had seen. The first son said that the tree was ugly, bent, and twisted. The second son said it was covered with green buds and full of promise. The third son said it was laden with blossoms that smelled so sweet and looked so beautiful. The last son said it was ripe and drooping with fruit, full of life and fulfillment. The man then explained to his sons that they were all right, because they had each seen only one season in the tree's life. He told them that you cannot judge a tree, or a person, by only one season, and that the essence of who they are and the pleasure, joy, and love that come from that life can only be measured when all the seasons are up. If you give up when it's winter, you will miss the promise of your spring, the beauty of your summer, the fulfillment of your fall.

I feel that I survived all four seasons with Philip. Spring was the time of joy and falling in love with an exciting man. Summer was when we made plans to change people's lives by creating SomaLife. Fall was a time of pain and withering in our lives. Winter was when Philip closed his eyes for the last time.

As I am now past the end of this chapter of my life—nearly at the fifth anniversary of Philip's death—I realize I never really grieved his loss, or any of the other losses that occurred throughout our time together. With the writing of this book, I visited my memory banks and allowed myself to acknowledge all that had transpired, and a huge wave of grief finally hit me like a tsunami. You can't change the past, but you can make your tomorrows brighter.

The following has been posted on the infidelity support website, which I am very thankful that I no longer need, and I feel it is both relevant for and important to my story. I apologize that I am unable to give credit to the author of this piece as no credit had been given:

If you are holding onto something that doesn't belong to you and was never intended for your life, then you need to LET IT GO.
If you are holding onto the past hurts and pains, LET IT GO.
If someone can't treat you right, love you back, and see your worth, LET IT GO.
If someone has angered you, LET IT GO.
If you are holding onto some thoughts of evil and revenge, LET IT GO.
If you are involved in a wrong relationship or addiction, LET IT GO.
If you are holding onto a job that no longer meets your needs or talents, LET IT GO.
If you have a bad attitude, LET IT GO.
If you keep judging others to make yourself feel better, LET IT GO.
If you're stuck in the past and God is trying to take you to a new level in Him, LET IT GO.

*If you are struggling with the healing of a broken relationship,
LET IT GO.
If you keep trying to help someone that will not help themselves,
LET IT GO.
If you are depressed and stressed, LET IT GO.
If there is a situation that you are so used to handling yourself
and God is saying "take your hands off of it," then LET IT GO.
Let the past be the past. Forget the former things and LET IT
ALL GO. You must take the good with the bad, smile with the
sad, love what you've got, and remember what you had. Always
forgive but never forget. People change, things go wrong. Just
remember this... life goes on.*

These are powerful words! It is not easy to forgive, especially because it means giving up all hope of a better past. But in the end, that is exactly what you need to do. Nothing will change the past—you can only move forward in whatever way works for you.

While SomaLife is now evolving into what it should have been so long ago, my life continues to be a series of twists and turns. About a month after our wonderful wedding, Bob went in for a physical exam and the doctor found an elevated PSA (prostate-specific antigen) reading. This didn't seem to be a big concern at the time as most men have prostate issues as they get older, so even though they did some additional testing we put it out of our minds. We went off on our week-long honeymoon to Mexico and had an amazing time. And when we returned, Bob was diagnosed with stage four prostate cancer. We were in shock. How could this be? Our life together had just started.

Unwilling to give up, we started doing research. By a stroke of luck, we spoke to our neighbour and found out that he also had prostate cancer. His wife had done a great deal of research and was able to get him on a clinical trial which really turned things around for him. We applied to have Bob join that clinical trial, and thankfully he was accepted. So far, the results are promising—a recent PSA test showed that his numbers were significantly lower than before.

One of the things I love about Bob is that he is pragmatic, and he hasn't let a little thing like cancer slow him down. He is still an amazing motorcycle instructor, and for the last three years he has been taking the police motorcycle riding course, which is more stringent than any course most riders would ever take. He is now qualified to train police riders himself.

Unfortunately, the twists and turns didn't stop there. Within a month of Bob being diagnosed with cancer, we got the news that Philip's son Andrew, whom we have remained very close with, was very ill. He sent us a note letting us know that he had been diagnosed with a cancerous brain tumour. The treatments for this condition caused his brain to swell, which then resulted in cancer-induced epilepsy. His career as an ace captain for Cathay Pacific was over, and he was struggling with both physical and cognitive symptoms. He wasn't even allowed to leave the house on his own in case he fell or had a seizure. The whole thing felt impossible. Andrew was only forty-seven years old and had always been active; he should still have had a lifetime ahead of him. I was glad that Philip was spared this devastating news.

Andrew made such a great choice when he married Jennine all those years ago. Even though she is the vice principal at an expat school in Hong Kong, she takes care of Andrew and their two children while maintaining her career. Even with this health crisis, both Andrew and Jennine find time to ask about Bob and how he is doing. I consider myself lucky to have them—as well as Phil Jr. and his family—as part of my life.

Nothing is guaranteed in life, and that became so evident in September of 2020, when Bob's middle son, Norman, and youngest son, Darren, both died peacefully in their sleep within two weeks of each other. Due to health issues, their hearts were not strong, and one day they just ceased to function. Dealing with two close family members' funerals in a matter of two weeks was almost too much to bear—in fact, it was inconceivable. Bob's grief was palpable, and there was little I could do but to be there for him.

I don't know what the future holds for any of us, but I know Bob will keep doing what he is doing. He is not one to feel sorry for himself, and for that I am thankful. We have many friends who will help see us through whatever comes our way. We will continue to make memories, because in the end that is all we have.

I also know that I will carry on Philip's legacy, and now mine, by continuing to promote Youth Formula, our flagship product. For all of the challenges we faced in our marriage, I truly believe that he was a brilliant man and that the product he created can change lives. Have a look at the testimonials I've included at the end of this book, and you'll see just how true this is. Everything that Philip accomplished in the past, along with the choices I have made to further the company, has led to a better future that I can pass down to his sons and their families.

And finally, I know that I will no longer be steamrolled by stronger opinions or told that I am not capable. I will not hand over the reins of my company to someone who claims they know best. I will set boundaries so that I can remain true to myself. I have found my voice and I am no longer afraid. I have come out of the shadows, and I will no longer let anyone try to hide my light.

Testimonial for Youth Formula

"I've been on Youth Formula for a month now and am feeling wonderful changes. I am losing inches, my facial sagging is improving, my digestion and bowels are improved, my psoriasis flared up...and is now healing and disappearing more and more...Youth Formula now seems to energize me."
—P.S., Anglemont, BC

***

"I have been on product approximately two months. Before I began, my left eye was covered in black spots whenever I blinked. Two diagnoses have indicated different things: a problem with my liver or perhaps a problem with upcoming blindness down the road. I now do not have to wonder which is the correct diagnosis as the spots are all gone! The other problem I had was sleep apnea...last night was the eighth night that I've slept through the night. Not once did I have to be woken up because I had stopped breathing...I am sleeping through the night for the first time in ages. What a great feeling!"
—V.T., Carp, ON

***

"I found my eyesight improved almost immediately. I went from needing low-strength reading glasses to none in about two weeks. After about one and a half to two months being on the product, I found my knees were no longer creaking and groaning when bending or standing. I have better energy overall and sleep quite well on a regular basis. I believe I will be on this product forever."

—J.S., Dawson Creek, BC

***

"Fluffy is twenty years old and is my daughter's Persian cat...had always been active...last year she began to spend more and more time indoors and was less active than she had been. About three weeks ago she began to lose her balance when she got up from her naps. Her eyes got kind of glazed and were not bright like they used to be. She was hardly eating at all and spent most of her time just dozing...she sometimes didn't quite get into the box to do her "business"...I noticed the weaving and loss of balance...I quickly took out a Youth Formula capsule and put some on a bit of food...I did this three times that day and have continued for the last two weeks. She now has eyes that are clear and focused, her litter box area is clean, and she has asked to go outdoors. Last night she ate only the portion with Youth Formula sprinkled on it, and she did the same thing this morning. She actually jumped on my lap yesterday while I was working on the computer! She had been too weak to do that for ages now."

—V.T., Carp, ON

***

"...[M]y heart rate has slowed down...It's amazing! When I did my aerobics yesterday, I breezed through it (and that's not normal). I haven't done anything exercise-wise in about two months. The ten-second count that is always at the end of the aerobics section was the most incredible evidence that something was different with my heart...I seemed to have lots of energy, I couldn't believe it was already over when I got to the end of the aerobic part of the tape. I've been on Youth Formula for five to six weeks...Good news for sure! Thank you for this product."
—H.C., Williams Lake, BC

***

"I began taking Youth Formula five months ago (May 15). My sister had called me from Maui way back in March to tell me about this great product that improves health, etc. I had no interest in looking at any more health products. I was already taking plenty of supplements and didn't really feel I needed to improve my health as much as I needed to improve the run-down antique house with a run-down antique store my husband and I had just purchased.

"Week after week, my sister told me, 'I'm taking "Youth" and I feel great!' The more she encouraged me (pressured me), the more I resisted, reminding her that I had never really been sick, only injured. Admittedly, very injured. I had broken my left leg water skiing twenty years ago (a tibial plateau fracture, so serious they almost amputated it), and my right leg ice-skating five years ago (a tibia-fibula spiral fracture, so serious it took close to two years to heal properly). They had inserted a metal plate and seven pins in my left leg (my x-ray looked just like the Eiffel Tower upside down), and four pins and a rod (which looks like a large piece of plumbing pipe) in my right leg. Though I had never been sick, I had undergone a total of six leg surgeries, which culminated in eventually getting ALL the metal out. I have been known to tote it around in a bag like a souvenir, and when I tell people it looks like I could erect a swing set with all that metal, they always agree. And whenever people swap war stories or compare battle scars, I usually win with my left knee. That knee will never be the same. So...injured, yes, but never sick.

"More than a month went by. My sister would say, 'I'm taking Soma and...' I would finish the sentence for her, 'I know. I know. You feel great.' It became a running joke with us. With her continued encouragement (pressure), I finally agreed to look at the Youth Formula, mostly so she would finally leave me alone. I tried to find things wrong with it. I told her there must be a reason why we stop producing HGH and that we probably should not tamper with nature. Then I found out we do not actually stop producing HGH at all, we simply gradually slow down releasing it as we age. There went that argument. I thought I had won when I told her that I was not interested in one of those 'here today, gone tomorrow' remedies. But the more I researched the subject, the more I realized there was nothing new-fangled or experimental about it. Since the beginning of time, HGH is, always was, and always will be responsible for the regeneration of our cells. I was starting to like this stuff. Though it was really starting to pique my interest, I still had to point out some of the dangers I had read about concerning HGH. As it turns out, other HGH products that make similar claims all contain animal extractions that do indeed make them dangerous. Youth Formula does not contain any animal extractions; it is pure food. I could hardly think of any more reasons NOT to try it. My final attempt:

I reminded her that I have a house to remodel and a shop to fill with antiques, and that I could not entertain the idea of spending so much money on a supplement. When I saw that the product costs approximately $2 per day and that it should be considered part of my food budget, I had run out of excuses. It was time to try it.

"The first night I took it, I slept as though someone had slipped me a sedative. I had not slept through the night since my daughter was born twelve years ago. My son, now nine, slept in my bed kicking me all night until he was six. And my husband has been managing a pub for the past three years, which has him coming home at 2:30 a.m., making himself omelets at 3:00 a.m., asking me if I want any omelets at 3:30 a.m., and finally coming to bed at 4:00. My alarm goes off at 5:00 a.m. How could I possibly sleep through the night?! I was a chronic mess, but I accepted it as my life and tried not to ever let a little fatigue slow me down! Against all odds, I did sleep through that first night taking Soma, missed my husband coming home, missed the whole omelet thing, and barely made it out of bed with my alarm clock.

"I woke up feeling groggy. During that day, I felt like I had ingested both a stimulant and a sedative; my head had a buzzing sensation, though the grogginess never totally abated. Night after night, I slept deeper and deeper. Day after day, I felt more and more like I was coming down with the flu. I could not remember what I was about to say and would leave sentences half finished. I had an unquenchable thirst that no amount of water could relieve.

"I had a metallic taste in my mouth so strong that it tasted like I had been sucking on a car battery (or how I imagine that might taste). I thought I had gotten all the metal out of my body; I thought I had been toting it around in a bag.

The phenomenon was both creepy and awesome. It would have been easy to throw the Youth Formula away and blame it for making me feel so awful, but I knew better. I knew enough about 'cleansing reactions' to ride this out even as the symptoms seemed to worsen. I developed an intermittent tingling sensation in my arms that reminded me ever so much of the way it feels when they put anesthesia into your arm with an IV. I had to assume that this sensation was residue from that same anesthesia now leaving my body! Perhaps that is why I felt half-looped. Perhaps I was half anesthetized!

"By the seventh and ninth days respectively, I had social commitments with close friends I chose not to cancel. Still in a fog, I apologized by letting them know I was amid detoxing. It must have appeared appealing in some bizarre way as they each asked me, 'How can I get some of that stuff?'

"These symptoms (mental confusion, metallic taste in my mouth, tingling sensation in my arms) continued for twelve days. And then one morning, I woke up and they were gone. They were replaced by a stabbing pain in my lower back (on the right side only), a pain so severe that I could not bend over to tie my shoes and had a hard time bending enough to get in and out of bed. I had no frame of reference for this pain and had to take a wild guess that my right kidney was struggling to filter out these toxins that had been pulled out of my cells. That pain lasted for three days (days twelve through fourteen).

"On the fifteenth morning, I woke up feeling as though nothing had happened. I felt great, but tired. I was sleeping like a little child, night after night. In fact, sleeping was my new hobby. I would cancel fun plans saying, 'I can't possibly go to that. I'm going to bed at 8:30!' More than once, I fell asleep with my face squished against my little clipboard, pen in hand, waiting for the SomaLife conference call that was to begin at

9:30 p.m. EST (Cape Cod time!). I was starving to get more information about this product and to learn more about what it was doing to my body, but the urge to sleep would overwhelm me. I had not remembered sleeping like that since high school!

"I continued to feel more tired than energetic for a total of three and a half months. Generally, I have always been extremely high energy; I never let my usual lack of sleep slow me down. But this was different! It took some adjusting to get used to this new lethargic pace. Thankfully, I knew that this fatigue and the cleansing symptoms from the first two weeks, though somewhat uncomfortable, were only temporary. I was not falling apart at the seams. I was excited and confident I would eventually come through this healthier, happier, and stronger (to say nothing of better rested), and come through it I did!

"I have just completed my fifth month taking Youth Formula. The improvements I am experiencing are all over the map, so here they are in no particular order. My energy level has rebalanced itself. I am sleeping great. My skin has improved, especially the dark circles under my eyes that I have had for thirty years. My blood sugar level used to drop and I would get shaky if I went for much more than three hours without eating; I have been running around the flea markets this summer/fall in pursuit of antiques, sometimes forgetting to eat for more than five hours without any hypoglycemic symptoms. I have an overall sense of well-being that is indescribable. My hair is definitely growing faster. At 105 pounds I was never overweight, but a bit sproinged from the pregnancy with my daughter, and especially my son (a ten-and-a-half-pound baby). Suddenly, my figure looked the way it used to before having children. Ironically, I gained three pounds but lost one pant size. I have never been accused of being mellow, but despite my high energy level I notice a distinct new sense of inner calm. The most remarkable of all is the improvement to the chronic pain in my left knee. I had been taking a sulfur product for close to three years that had greatly reduced the pain. Youth Formula seems to have taken it away! In fact, it has taken it away to the degree I tweaked my knee bounding up the stairs two at a time the other day, forgetting that I really do still need to favour it. I am sure there are other improvements, just as I am sure there are others yet to come.

"By no means do I deign to walk around saying, 'I am healed! I am rejuvenated! It only took five months for Youth Formula to work, and now it has and so now everything is just great!' I do not see it like that at all, mostly because I realize that healing (rejuvenation) is a gradual and continual process, not an encapsulated event that takes a certain number of months to accomplish. But I do feel confident that Youth Formula has enabled me to begin that process in a way that far surpasses anything I had anticipated.

"And to think it all began with a detoxification I was grossly unaware I needed! I had no reason to believe I was toxic; I have NEVER smoked, NEVER done recreational drugs, and only RARELY had wine or German beer (I am quite selective!). My sister and I grew up with a mother who was a true nutrition devotee, and for as long as I can remember we have been into whole foods, food combining, natural supplements, herbs, juicing, fasting, colonics, dry brush massage, and every form of internal and external cleansing you can think of. If you had told me MY cells were polluted, I would not have believed you. Is it any wonder that I am so amazed at Youth Formula's ability to pull these insidious toxins out of my cells like no other supplement or modality ever had or could have? Thank goodness YF enhances the body's INNATE healing intelligence on a cellular level. No matter how 'intelligent' I felt my health and nutrition choices had always been, I never could have accomplished such positive benefits in so little time, or EVER for that matter!

"My heart goes out to the skeptic. I empathize with the person who is too busy, too distracted, too unimpressed, or just plain-old too stubborn to try this. It is amazing to me to think that I almost did not try this product. I was infinitely more focused on renovating my house rather than tending to a greatly needed renovation of my body! As stated, I had no idea what a walking medical waste dump (for metal, anesthesia, x-ray, toxins) I had become. No, I had never been sick, but I shudder to think of just how sick I was destined to become down the road. I am so thankful I ran out of excuses NOT to try it.

"The improvements I have recounted have all made a substantial difference in the quality of my life. Some are subtle. Some are ASTOUNDING! Now I can honestly tell people, 'I'm taking Youth Formula and I feel GREAT!' I am grateful to my sister for encouraging me, as I now encourage anyone who wants to listen. Youth Formula is worth trying. And with that, I wish those who do try it the best of luck and the best of health."

—T.C., Cape Cod, MA

***

"We love the many positive testimonials we continuously receive from the people we now see as members of the SomaLife Family. And now, I would like to offer my own testimonial as well.

"When we started the company in 1998, I had just turned fifty. I was the first to start on the product and I referred to myself as the company guinea pig. I immediately felt more energy and was able to do many strenuous tasks with quicker recovery. I had joined a dragon boat team in 2000, and as steerer I had to physically control a boat loaded with twenty paddlers, a drummer, and myself with only a long oar. It was very intense, but I felt that I was able to do this better and recover faster once I began taking Youth Formula. I slept better, my nails became stronger, and my hair grew quicker and was not turning white. There were so many benefits to how I felt. I believed Philip when he told me that my body was getting the wonderful benefits of full body cell repair. He would often say, 'It goes in and fixes what needs fixing.' What a simple concept."

—Marlies

Author Biography

At the age of fifty, Marlies was enjoying an active lifestyle as a dragon boater, pilot, car racer, scuba diver, RCMP Auxillary, and more.

She was reluctant to give any of this up due to "getting old," so she encouraged her husband to formulate a product that would slow the effects of aging, In 1998, she started SomaLife in the basement of their home to produce their patented Youth Formula. The company has always been her baby, and she is passionate about being able to provide affordable world-class supplements to as many people as possible. She is active in her community, especially with the local food bank. The company's SomaPet supplement was specifically created because of her love of animals, and incidentally it was tested on humans.

To this day, Marlies is proof of the benefits of this incredible product. She purchased her first Harley Davidson at the age of sixty-nine and rode with the Military Police National Motorcycle Relay at the age of seventy-one to raise funds for blind children in Canada.

And now, at age seventy-two, she continues to live a full and active life by staying young as old as possible. Knowing how important her company is, she looks forward to fulfilling her husband's legacy, and her own, in the coming years. She is a Best Selling co-author of two of the Woman of Worth collaborative books.

www.somalife.com
www.facebook.com/marlieswhite
www.linkedin.com/in/marlies-white-61191653/
twitter.com/Marlies_White
www.facebook.com/somalifehealth/
www.theisfp.com/members-2/marliessomalife-com/profile/
www.instagram.com/whitemarlies/

Acknowledgements

I could dedicate a full chapter to all the people I want to thank, for the many ways you have all helped to inspire me in bringing this book to becoming a reality. Heartfelt thanks to all my RockStars!

To my publisher, Julie Salisbury, who encouraged me to tell my story; for all your support and helping me launch my book from your casa in Mexico.

To my editor, Danielle Anderson, and typesetter Greg Salisbury, and my graphic artist, Tara Eymundson, who have all brought my book into the light.

To Kim Roberts, who works tirelessly in the SomaLife office and makes me look good, and Brenda Lemoin, who keeps the company on track with her financial expertise.

To Dr. Charlyn Belluzzo, who provides me with medical-professional support, and helps keep our customers informed of newsworthy health information.

To my family and closest friends who have never doubted that I could do this and have always had my back.

And especially to Robert Gemmell Smith, my husband and best friend. You have sacrificed time together to allow me to write this book. I could not have done this without your belief in me, or your unquestioning support. I know you love me, and I am grateful with this new chapter of my life.